THE RIGHT WAY TO
RIDE
A
HORSE

W. H. Walter's

THE RIGHT WAY TO
RIDE
A
HORSE

Revised and edited by
Hugh Venables

A PAPERFRONT
ELLIOT RIGHT WAY BOOKS
KINGSWOOD, SURREY, U.K.

Conditions of sale
This book shall only be sold, lent or hired for profit, trade, or otherwise
In its original binding, except where special permission has been granted
by the Publishers.
Every effort is made to ensure that paperfronts and Right Way Books
are accurate, and that the information given in them is correct.
However, information can become out of date, and author's or
printer's errors can creep in. This book is sold, therefore, on the
condition that neither Author nor Publisher can be held legally
responsible for the consequences of any error or omission there may be.

Set, printed and bound in Great Britain by
Cox & Wyman Ltd, Reading

Contents

List of Illustrations

Introduction

Riding horses is a most enjoyable pastime. It is carried out in the open-air, in pleasant surroundings, and it offers an opportunity to escape completely from the workaday routine of school, home or job.

As an exercise, riding is also useful, and to people of all ages. It brings into play practically all the muscles of the human trunk and limbs, and it also calls for a co-ordination of mind and action which is most beneficial. Riding a horse encourages the rider to learn to make quick decisions, and it teaches him to keep his temper and handle the horse with patience and tact. Moreover, successful management of the horse can endow those who naturally lack it with considerable confidence.

But, most of all, riding horses is fun. A book describing the right way to go about it must, necessarily, be instructive rather than entertaining, but this does not mean that the whole business of learning to ride is a solemn ritual. It is not: riding is a sociable, pleasant sport and, while sensible safety precautions should not be neglected, its main object is to enjoy association with 'that great gentleman, the horse'.

1

Psychology of Horse and Rider

In all our dealings with the horse it must be remembered that he is a highly strung animal, sensitive and quick to react to signals which the rider may not even have noticed. This helps to explain why horses do some of the apparently quite irrational things they do. It also explains why the rider's own temperament can have such a surprising effect on a horse, nervousness and fear being communicated particularly easily. Thus it is plain that if, in all our dealings with him, we approach the horse in a quiet, gentle, yet confident, manner we shall achieve the best results.

The horse is a sociable, friendly animal and has adapted himself to human company remarkably well over a few thousand years of domestication. He is usually willing to please, if only he can understand what is wanted of him – though in the matter of interpreting human signals he can often be unbelievably dim.

His fears may at times seem very great, and quite irrational, too, but they are part of the instinct of self-preservation which is so strong in the horse. Allied to this is his basic tendency to escape from danger – real or imagined – by his fleetness of foot; the blind panic and unreasoned galloping of a frightened horse is evidence of this.

The Horse is Friendly

Once these characteristics of the horse are understood it is seen that any fears we may have harboured in connection with him are groundless. It is very rare indeed to find a horse that deliberately tries to hurt people, though it should be remembered that the horse does not realize his own strength and weight – as those who have placed their toes under a horse's foot will testify.

So, if you would establish a *détente* with the horse you are to ride, approach him sympathetically, and you will have to accept that he is not a wild, vicious animal, but then neither is he a machine. A good guide in your treatment of him is to consider him as a sensitive, yet highly strung, child; he must not be allowed to get away with too much, but he will not necessarily understand all you 'say' to him – but then developing a perfect understanding with the horse is what learning to ride is all about.

2

Know Your Horse

Before beginning your first riding lesson you will find it
helpful and instructive to walk round the stables and have a
look at the horses. This will give you an idea of the animals'
general attitude to life, and you will notice that individual
horses seem to vary in temperament and outlook almost as
much as people do.

Making the acquaintance of the horse you are to ride is
also useful; you will probably find that he is kindly disposed
and in a few minutes you will have introduced yourself to
him. This will make it that much easier to make some communication with the animal when you mount.

You must remember when handling horses that they are
easily frightened, so always approach an animal quietly and
confidently, and avoid shouting or making sudden noises.
Beware of being too quiet though – if you creep up on a
horse unawares you may well make him jump out of his
skin, which is not the best foundation for friendship! A few
words of greeting are a great help.

Another thing to consider in your dealings with the horse
is that he can see almost all round his body, and that he can
also locate very accurately with those mobile ears the source
of any sound, so always move unhurriedly, and let the horse
know where you are and what you are doing.

The majority of horses enjoy being patted and stroked,
particularly on the neck; don't pat a horse on the head and
nose, though – he won't like it (well, would you?), and also
be careful about handling his ears, for some animals resent
this. For most horses part of the charm of being petted lies
in the possibility of an accompanying tit-bit, and some deli-

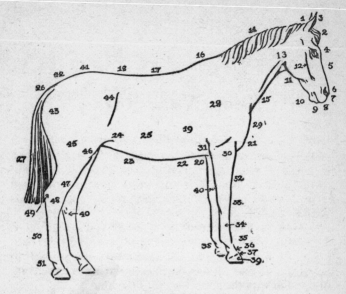

FIG 1. THE POINTS OF THE HORSE

Head and Neck
1. Poll.
2. Forelock.
3. Ears.
4. Forehead.
5. Face.
6. Muzzle.
7. Nostrils.
8. Upper Lip.
9. Lower Lip.
10. Chin Groove.
11. Lower Jaw.
12. Cheekbone.
13. Gullet.
14. Mane (Crest).
15. Windpipe.

Body
16. Withers.

17. Back.
18. Loins.
19, 25. Rib Cage (barrel).
20. Girth Place.
21. Breast.
22. Floor of Chest.
23. Belly.
24. Flank.

Tail
26. Dock.
27. Hair of Tail.

Limbs and Croup
28. Shoulder.
29. Point of Shoulder.
30. Foreleg.
31. Elbow.
32. Forearm.

33. Knee.
34. Cannon Bone.
35. Fetlock Joint.
36. Pastern.
37. Coronet.
38. Heels.
39. Hoof.
40. Chestnut.
41. Haunch.
42. Croup.
43. Hip Joint.
44. Point of Hip.
45. Upper Thigh.
46. Stifle.
47. Lower Thigh.
48. Hock.
49. Point of Hock.
50. Tendon (of hindleg).
51. Ergot.

cacy, such as crust of bread (no butter) or a piece of apple will be much appreciated.

Preparing to Mount

Having made friends with the horse from the safety of ground-level, we have to think about how we are going to cope when we are on his back. It is natural for most of us, when we are embarking on something new, to want to be sure that we can stop when we wish. This is true of riding too and it is a common fear that one's horse will get going, and then one will be unable to slow him down, and he will just go faster and faster . . . But you really need not worry on this account, for most horses really are very obliging and willingly obey a clear command to steady up. Moreover, no instructor would put a complete beginner on any but the most quiet, reliable horse who is well used to the ways of the learner rider. So really there is nothing to fear in these first lessons, you can settle down and enjoy them and, if you are considerate to him, your horse shouldn't find them too arduous either.

Before you make your first attempts at mounting the horse, watch how he is brought from the stable; he is turned gently, and care is taken that he does not knock himself on the door jambs. Remember that, once outside the stable, the horse must always be held, either by the reins or by a head-collar and rope, so that there is no risk of his departing on his own should he take fright. The headcollar, incidentally, is a piece of stable equipment, a harness of leather, nylon straps or rope that fits the animal's head, but has no bit so that he can, if necessary, wear it all the time. The headcollar and attached rope are of sufficient strength to withstand the horse's pulling back if he is tethered, in a stall, for instance, or a horse-box. The bridle is not designed to withstand stresses of this sort, so that horses should never be tied up by their reins.

When you go for your riding lesson and just mount the ready-saddled horse that is led out of the stable for you, you do not realize how much skill and work is entailed in keeping the horse fit and well. Careful feeding, grooming, the business of mucking out the stable and the cleaning the saddlery, rugging up the animal in winter, shoeing and care of the horse's feet, and organizing regular exercise are all involved. But these tasks, by and large, are not unpleasant and many are great fun. More and more people are embarking on the business of looking after the horse as well as riding it, either by enjoying trekking holidays where they care for their own mounts for a week or so, or by taking the plunge and getting a horse of their own. Either way, the amount of pleasure you derive from your riding is really related to just how well you know your horse.

3

How to Describe a Horse

To distinguish one horse from another, a combination of its
size, colour, breed and sex is used to describe him (or her).
Most of the terms used are peculiar to horsey parlance and
may take some getting used to as they have evolved over
many years and the logic behind many of them has been lost
long ago. It is worthwhile having some knowledge of what
the most common words mean before you embark on your
riding career, or you may find that a strange statement like
'You're to ride the blue roan in the back box, the one with
the snip and star' quite mystifying!

Let us begin by considering the sex of horses. A female
horse is a 'filly foal' until she reaches one year of age, when
she is called just a 'filly'. She remains a filly until she is
mature, at about three years of age, when she becomes a
mare, and this she is for the rest of her life.

A male horse is a 'colt foal' until he is a year old, when he
becomes a 'colt'. For riding and most general purposes male
horses are usually castrated at about one year old to make
them more docile, and they are then called 'geldings'; a 'rig'
or 'cryptorchid' is a male horse which has been incompletely
castrated and shows some of the wildness of the uncastrated
'stallion' or 'horse'. A 'rig' will generally have to undergo a
more serious operation to complete the castration, when he
should become as docile as any other gelding.

Size of Horses

The size of a horse is stated in 'hands' (one hand being four
inches) and inches. It is measured with a graduated stick
which stands vertically on the ground beside the horse's

withers and has a cross-bar which rests on the withers. This is fitted with a spirit level so that it can be adjusted to be perfectly horizontal. The animal's height is measured to the highest point of its withers and is stated as, for example, 'fourteen hands and one inch' which means that the pony is in fact 57 inches tall.

Technically, a horse (nothing to do with its sex now) is an animal over 14 hands and 2 inches in height and a pony is below this size. A polo pony is, however, called a pony for traditional reasons, whatever its size, and a horse of the Arab breed is always a horse, though it may not be over 14.2 H.H.

The matter of what size or type of animal is a 'cob' often perplexes novice riders, too, for the term can have a variety of meanings. As a type, the cob is a short-legged stocky animal, described as 'the body of a horse on the legs of a pony', and 'cobby' describes these characteristics. 'Cobsize', on the other hand, has a rather different meaning as far as saddlery is concerned for it is the middle of the three common sizes in which harness and horse-clothing is made, 'full-size' or 'horse', 'cob' and 'pony'. In this context the 'cob' size covers animals from about 13.2 H.H. to 15 hands.

Breed and Type

There are a number of breeds of horses and ponies, plus innumerable cross-breds, and it is unnecessary to go into all of them here (see Walter's Horse Keeper's Encyclopedia, a companion book in the same series). Some explanation of one or two of the more unexpected terms is required though, otherwise they could initially confuse you.

A Thoroughbred horse (with a capital T) is one whose ancestry can be traced back on both sides to horses entered in the General Stud Book. The G.S.B. itself was first published in 1791 when the Thoroughbred had become established as a result of crossing fine eastern horses with the native British stock. The Thoroughbred (or TB) has been bred for many years for speed and athletic ability and not only are all racehorses of this breed but also a large proportion of the horses used for competitive events such as combined training (three day events) and similar work. The Thoroughbred influence is even wider, as the breed has been crossed extensively with heavier stock to give lightness and speed in riding horses, show-jumpers and hunters.

The term 'Thoroughbred' or 'blood horse' should not be confused with 'pure bred', which is applied to horses and animals of other particular breeds. Examples are the pure bred Welsh Mountain pony, Exmoor pony or Cleveland Bay horse, and there are many more. The Breed Societies keep their own stud books, and pure bred animals are registered by them.

Colours of horses

The colour of a horse is used to describe it, both officially and casually. Horses are not generally ear-marked as cattle and pigs are so that an accurate description of colour and markings becomes important in distinguishing one horse from another, for example, for legal purposes.

The colour of a horse's body may be described by the following terms.

Bay – the horse has a brown or tan body with a black mane and tail and, almost invariably, black on his legs.

Black – this is self-explanatory, the horse being black all over except for any white markings; his muzzle must also be black.

Brown – Basically this means that the horse is dark brown all over, but the term would also describe a horse which is black except for a brown muzzle.

Chestnut – a tannish or yellowish colour varying in intensity to the 'liver chestnut' which is the darkest chestnut and is the colour of cooked liver. The mane and tail of a chestnut is the same colour as the rest of his body, or a little lighter.

Roan – implies a permanent ground colour on the body with an admixture of white hairs. A 'blue roan' is basically black or blackish brown, a 'red roan' bay or bay-brown and a 'strawberry roan' chestnut with the scattered white hairs giving the blue, red or strawberry tinge respectively.

Grey – Though horses can range from almost pure white to a dark pewter colour these would seldom be called anything but 'grey'. All grey horses have dark skins (which differentiates them from cream horses which have pink skins, creamy coats, tails and manes, and often eyes with blue or pink irises ('wall-eyes').

Dun – Like greys, dun horses have black skins, but they also have black manes and tails. Their coats are pale, yellowish or creamy in colour, sometimes a mixture of golden hairs with darker ones giving a bluish appearance. A dun may have a 'seal stripe' or 'list' – a dark stripe running the length of his backbone.

Piebald horses have large, irregular patches of black and white, and their manes and tails may also be parti-coloured.

Skewbalds have large irregular patches of any definite colour but black.

Markings

Many 'whole-coloured' horses, that is, of colours other than piebald or skewbald, have white markings, particularly on their heads. A 'star' is a small, white mark on the horse's forehead, and it may be extended down the animal's face as a 'stripe', which is no more than about 2 inches wide, and centrally placed. A wider area of white down the horse's face is a 'blaze', which covers most of his forehead. A 'snip' is a small, isolated white marking situated in the region of the horse's nostrils.

When the lower parts of the limbs are white, straightforward description such as 'white pastern' (white from just below the fetlock downards) or 'white fetlock' (white from below the knee downards) is less ambiguous and really to be preferred to the more traditional 'sock' and 'stocking' respectively.

Most other terms in general use for describing horses' colours are self-explanatory, 'spotted' or 'zebra-striped', for example. The presence of an animal's mane and tail is usually mentioned in descriptions, the latter for traditional reasons since it has been illegal to dock horses (except for veterinary reasons, such as serious injury to the tail, when the operation must be performed by a veterinary surgeon) for some years now. Manes may, however, be removed with clippers since they are as devoid of feeling as one's own hair; the process is known as 'hogging'.

The age of a horse is also used for description and identification since, with practice, it is reasonably easy to tell from the animal's teeth, and rather hard for the unscrupulous to conceal. By using all these characteristics a description is possible such as – 'Hercules. Bay Thoroughbred gelding, 8 years old, 15.3 H.H. He has a small star and a snip in his left nostril and both hind pasterns are white; he also has a white patch about 4 inches by 3 on his nearside at the girthmark. Mane and tail on.'

From such a description that horse could readily be picked out in a crowd, and the chances of another being identical are very slim.

4

Learning to Mount

Before you can begin your riding lesson you must get yourself into the saddle, and this apparently simple operation calls for quite a little explanation.

For your first attempts a dummy horse fitted with saddle and bridle is ideal but, failing this, a patient live animal, well used to the curious antics of learners is best. Don't forget, though, that even the most placid of animals can take fright unexpectedly, so it is wise to find a sympathetic human who will hold the horse's head, and perhaps give you a helping hand too. During these first attempts to get astride your steed it is easy to make a fool of yourself – but remember that that goes for everyone else too, and even the most proficient of horsemen can look back with a smile at the idiotic things they did during their first encounters with horses.

Before you try to mount, the stirrup leathers should be adjusted as nearly as possible to suit your height and enable you to get into the saddle without too much difficulty. The method usually adopted for gauging approximately the correct length of the stirrups is to place the bottom of the stirrup iron under your armpit and measure the length of the leathers against your outstretched arm; with the leather taut your knuckle should just touch the metal bar by which the stirrups are attached to the saddle. This, obviously, is only a rough guide as the relative lengths of arms and legs vary so much in different people.

It is usual to mount from the left or near (nearest the kerb) side, though later you should practise mounting from the off-side as well. Begin by standing beside the horse's left shoulder, facing his tail. Take up the reins between thumb and forefinger of your right hand and slide your left hand down the near-side rein as far as the withers, which is the name for that slightly higher portion of the horse's spine just in front of the saddle. Insert the two middle fingers of your left hand between the reins, passing the ends between thumb and forefinger, and drop the spare end to the off-side of the horse, in front of the saddle so that you do not find yourself sitting on it.

A word here about the 'feel' or pressure on the horse's mouth. A hard pull on the reins will hurt the horse and make him fidget, so that while you are learning to mount it is best to rely on a helper to hold the horse still; it is particularly important that you never use the reins to haul yourself into the saddle, something which it is surprisingly easy to do without realizing. Later, when you have become proficient at mounting, you will be able to maintain the steady gentle pressure on the horse's mouth that is necessary to make him stand still while you spring nimbly into the saddle. It is worth remembering that the off-side rein should be a fraction shorter than the other so that, should the horse attempt to turn, he can only turn his head away from you, thus both avoiding a playful nip where it hurts most from a mischievous horse, and also preventing the horse from moving his body away.

The mount

Once correctly positioned beside the horse's shoulder the next step is to take the stirrup leather in your right hand, just above the stirrup iron, and twist it so that the upper surface of the leather faces forward. Place your left foot in the stirrup iron, being careful at all times to push your toe downward so that you avoid digging it into the horse's side, which he will understandably resent. With your left hand – still, of course, holding the reins – grasp a lock of the mane at the withers or, in the absence of a mane, grasp the horse's neck and with your right hand hold the pommel of the saddle (the pommel is the front part of the saddle, pronounced 'pummel', as far over to the right side as possible. Many people grasp the cantle (or back) of the saddle but this tends to make the saddle slip round, makes the rider's position less secure and will eventually lead to distortion of the 'tree' or framework on which the saddle is built.

The position will now be as follows: your right hand grasps the pommel of the saddle; your left, with the reins

FIG. 2. MOUNTING

The rider has put her left foot in the stirrup and has hopped round directly facing, and close to, the saddle. Her right arm is placed across the seat to grasp the offside of the saddle below the pommel and she is ready to spring from the right foot.

preventing any forward movement of the horse, holds his neck while your left knee is pressed against the saddle and your left toe points downwards, against the girth. Your only contact with Mother Earth, therefore, is through the toe of your right foot. Now spring up from the right toe, avoiding as much as possible any tendency to pull up at the expense of the saddle, and at the same time straighten your left leg. This will bring you to a position where both legs are together close to the side of the horse, your body upright, and your weight borne by the near-side stirrup iron and supported to some extent by your hands.

Swing your right leg over the saddle, and allow your weight to come into the seat of the saddle gently – never land with a bump. Now place your right foot in the stirrup (in time you will learn to find the stirrup without looking down) and you are there.

A common mistake, made even by those riders who would consider themselves reasonably proficient, is to twist the stirrup leather the wrong way. The leather should be turned so that the under surface that lies next to the saddle is facing forward; this way the leather's edge will not dig into the rider's leg. If the unfortunate beginner is faced with a tall horse, it may help to let down the nearside leather a couple of holes, which are taken up again when you are mounted; alternatively, a mounting block may be used. Either could avoid ungainly stretching and perhaps that sharp, rending, sound that says that something has 'gone'!

Mounting without stirrups

Mounting without stirrups is certainly possible for the moderately athletic, with or without a saddle. The rider stands facing the horse's side, his left hand holding the reins and gripping the pommel of the saddle or the horse's neck, the other hand resting on the animal's back or the cantle of the saddle. Now press downwards with both hands and spring up, raising your body above the saddle: move your right hand forward, swing your right leg over the horse, and come gently into the saddle.

FIG. 3.   A HELPING HAND

'Getting a leg-up': This is a method of mounting with assistance, useful for a short rider with a tall horse. The rider faces the saddle, her left hand with the reins in front of the pommel, right hand on the seat of the saddle. She bends her left leg, holding it stiffly parallel with the ground, and her assistant places his left hand beneath the rider's knee and his right beneath her ankle. The rider now presses down with her arms and springs from her right toe as the assistant lifts. The rider then swings her right leg over the horse, placing her right hand on the off-side of the pommel of the saddle.

With practice, and practice is the essential part, the apparently complicated business of mounting the horse – with or without stirrups – can be readily mastered. The next step is to consider what you do once you are safely on the horse's back.

5

Your Seat on a Horse

As far as the seat is concerned riding is a combination of balance and grip. Correct balance, aided when necessary by grip, keeps the rider steady and firm in the saddle whatever the horse may do. One often hears a horseman spoken of as 'part of his horse'; such a rider has a perfectly balanced seat on the horse.

You must understand completely what is meant by a 'balanced seat'. It is the position on the horse which, entirely independent of reins or stirrups and without conscious grip by the legs, enables you to remain securely and easily in the saddle without unwillingly interfering with the movements of the horse. At the same time you are able to apply correctly and efficiently the 'aids' by which he is directed and controlled.

How can such a seat be developed?

The best way to approach the subject is to take the parts of the body in order and see what their various positions and functions are.

The seat bones

There is one place – and one place only – where the rider is intended to sit in the saddle, and that is in its lowest part. Sitting anywhere else inevitably leads to insecurity and makes it impossible for the rider to keep his body steady over his seat. The importance of sitting down in the saddle cannot be over-stressed. The weight of the rider is carried by his seat bones and by his thighs, relatively little being taken by the stirrups.

The thighs

The thighs can, when required, exert a very strong grip, but again no conscious grip is necessary with them; obviously in the action of rising at the trot no thigh grip can be maintained, the weight being carried by the knees and stirrups during the phase when your seat is out of the saddle.

Normally, the thighs are turned inwards so that their flat surfaces rest against the saddle. Those people who have very rounded thighs may find it easier to place them correctly if

FIG. 4.   THE SEAT

The 'balanced seat'. The rider's weight is so placed that her centre of gravity is on a vertical line passing through her body from head to heels and coinciding with the horse's centre of gravity; only thus can horse and rider be as one.

they pull the large muscle at the back of the thigh away from the saddle and to the rear, so ensuring that the flat of the thigh is correctly placed against the saddle, ready to exert any pressure or grip when it is needed. A guide to the position of the thighs is that for normal riding they should be at an angle of 45 degrees to the ground; this point often escapes the beginner. However, sitting the right way in the saddle, with the lower legs correctly placed, the thighs will automatically assume the proper position.

The lower legs

The lower legs – that is the part from the knee to the ankle – should hang naturally, with the ball of the foot in the stirrup and the stirrup leathers hanging vertically. Thus the lower part of the shin, the ankle and the heel lie slightly behind the perpendicular so that, on glancing down, you can only just see, or indeed cannot see at all, the tips of your toes beyond your knees. In this position a line drawn from toes to knees would be vertical.

Your legs provide you with your most valuable means of directing the horse and you cannot have full use of your legs, nor can you expect security of tenure, if your stirrups are not the right length. Adjusting the stirrups to the correct length will require some advice from your instructor but, as a general guide, sit in the saddle in as nearly the correct position as you can, but with your legs dangling out of the stirrup irons. Then adjust the stirrups so that the bottom of the irons are at the level of your ankle bone. At this length you will find that if you stand up with your weight carried on stirrups and knees the fork will just clear the pommel of a general purpose type saddle. As he learns to sit deeper in the saddle the novice rider may find that he has to let down his stirrups a little.

For some purposes stirrups are used longer or shorter than as described for general riding and hacking. The flat-race jockey is an extreme example, crouching forward over the horse's withers, but for jumping most riders will find it necessary to shorten the leathers a hole or two.

Altering the length of the stirrup leathers while in the saddle is not difficult, though it is surprising what a muddle some people get into. Before attempting to mount, your leathers will have been adjusted roughly to your height to allow you to mount without difficulty. Keep your feet in the irons and hold the loose end in one hand while the forefinger guides the tongue of the buckle. Remember, of course, to hold the reins in the other hand meanwhile, suitably lengthened to avoid making the horse step back while keeping adequate contact with his mouth. When your stirrups have been adjusted as required pull the under leathers downwards so that the buckle is brought up close to the bar again. The loose end may be tucked under the rest of the leathers from the front, but some people find the resulting bulge rather uncomfortable and prefer to let the end hang loose.

When the stirrups are properly adjusted and you are sitting correctly on your horse you will realize that they are provided mainly for convenience and comfort, and not to help you retain your seat in the saddle. Your calves should remain free to move and apply pressure (never a kick) to the horse. But remember never to grip with your calves as pressure just behind the horse's girth is the signal to which he responds by moving forward (equal pressure on both sides) or sideways (pressure on the side from which he is to move, applied a little further back). Some horses, particularly the placid type selected for the novice, may not respond very readily to the rider's leg; here turning the heels inwards towards the horse's sides may be helpful.

The feet

The heels should be pressed well down and the toes kept up, some pressure being maintained on the stirrup irons through the ball of the foot. Otherwise, the position of the feet is natural, as in walking, and more or less parallel with the horse's sides with the toes if anything turned very slightly outwards. Do not exaggerate this, though, for nothing looks more unsightly, and with feet continually at right angles to the horse's sides it becomes impossible to keep the insides

of the knees close to the saddle. It also brings the heels into
constant and unnecessary contact with the horse's sides.

The knees

The knees should remain still and snug against the saddle
flap, observably bearing weight only when the rider rises at
the trot or adopts a forward position over a fence or at a
canter or gallop.

The trunk and head

Having established the lower part of your body in a relaxed,
comfortable and – we hope – correct position you must realize that your back and head also play a very important
part in deciding whether you have a good or bad seat on a
horse. Your back should be straight and hollowed but not
stiff, with your shoulders back in a natural position. Your
head should be held high, looking straight in front and
neither tilted forward nor inclined to one side. For all its
straightness, your body should be supple and ready to give
sympathetically to the movements of the horse. Relaxation
and sympathy should not, however, be confused with a sagging posture, crouching over the reins with the head
bowed.

The arms

The upper arms should hang easily, with elbows close to the
body. The forearm lies across the body so that the hands
are some 4 inches apart. From the side, there should appear
to be a straight line running from your elbow through your
hands and the reins to the horse's mouth, and this is maintained whatever the position of the horse's head. The hands
are not fixed and fingers, wrists, elbows and shoulder joints
should all be ready to respond to the movements of the
horse's head.

It is difficult to describe the correct way to sit on a horse,
and on paper the whole business seems very complicated. In
practice it is a natural process, the rider sitting more easily,
and riding more effectively, as time goes on. As in all things

connected with the horse, the keynote in the establishment of a good position and seat on a horse is moderation, and – of course – practice. The practice is endless, and the horseman never stops learning about horses and improving his riding.

6

Your Hands on the Reins

As the reins are one of the chief means of communication
with the horse we are riding the importance of their correct
use cannot be too greatly stressed.

The bridle

Bridles and bits are of many different types, to be described in more detail later. For the time being let us consider only the basic snaffle bridle, a simple and effective
device and probably more common than all the other sorts
of bits and bridles put together.

The snaffle bit consists essentially of a metal mouthpiece,
usually jointed in the middle, and with a large ring at either
end. The bit is held in position in the animal's mouth by
means of a headstall which passes over the top of his head
behind his ears and is attached to the bit ring on either side
of his mouth. The headstall is kept in place by means of a
loop, the browband, across the horse's forehead and an adjustable throatlash round his gullet; there may also be a
noseband. The headstall is adjustable and the bridle fitted
so that the bit lies comfortably in the horse's mouth without
wrinkling his lips.

The reins are attached to the bit rings, so that a pull on
them exerts direct pressure on the horse's mouth. It should
be remembered that the joint in the middle of the snaffle
gives this bit a nutcracker-like action, with the horse's lower
jaw effectively the nut, and for all its apparent simplicity it is
quite a severe bit and to be used gently.

The bit actually presses on a delicate part of the sensitive
mouth; how sad it is that so many horses must undergo the

painful process of having the sensory nerves of the skin covering the inside of their lower jaws (the 'bars' of the mouth) and part of their tongues destroyed by riders' heavy handling of the reins. Once these nerves are destroyed the horse's mouth is numbed and sensitivity can never be regained – perhaps fortunately for the horse, for he suffers no more discomfort from ham-fisted riders.

So the need for gentleness in handling the reins should always be remembered. This does not mean just letting them hang loose, but rather maintaining a continual but very light and responsive 'feel' of the horse's mouth. The horse is trained throughout his life on the basis of correction and reward, and this goes for any sort of ridden work too; a direction is given the horse through the reins, and the reward for obeying is immediately to 'give' with the hand (the same principle applies to the aids which you give with your legs as well). Pain in his mouth will breed fear in a horse, which will make him fight and pull at the bit; he has not the intelligence to work out that if he stopped pulling so might his nervous, novice, rider – so it is up to you to make the first conciliatory advances!

How to hold the reins

You have learnt how to hold the reins in one hand for mounting; now you must take them into both hands, simply by transferring the right rein to your right hand so that you have one rein in each hand. Your thumbs are upwards and the rein passes from the horse's mouth to your knuckle, entering your partially closed hand between the third and little fingers and then running upwards across the palm of your hand. The grasp on the rein need not be tight, and you should use your fingers as well as your wrists to give you that sympathetic 'feel' of the horse's mouth.

Your wrists remain flexible and slightly flexed, but only enough to make the fingernails point towards the rider; if your wrists are too rounded they can only give – there is no room left for take.

Shortening the reins

On various occasions as, for example, when you begin to trot and the horse's head is held higher and closer to his body than it is when he is walking, it will be found necessary to shorten the reins in order to maintain contact with the horse's mouth. With the reins held in one hand this is very simple. Just take the loop end in your right hand and draw the reins through the fingers of your left until they are the required length. With the reins held in both hands the simplest way is to transfer the reins to your left hand, shorten them as just described, and then replace your right hand in its correct position on the rein.

Both these ways are very straightforward, and may seem hardly worth describing, but during early lessons shortening the reins can be surprisingly difficult. The most common tendency is for the novice rider to try and edge his hands forward along the reins one at a time, not infrequently ending up by dropping both.

Remember always to keep your hands down, and never lift them up in order to see what you are doing. I know you will say 'That's silly, as if I would!' – but you would be surprised! Anyway, why look at your hands at all? Even so, you may find yourself doing it without thinking, much as a person learning to drive a car has a most disconcerting habit of looking down at the controls, instead of at the road ahead.

7

The Aids:
Instructions to Your Horse

The 'aids' are the means by which your wishes are conveyed to the horse, and you must be capable of using them independently of each other, or of combining them, as required. We know already that the hands, signalling via the reins to the horse's mouth, are one of the 'aids'; in addition the rider uses his legs and slight changes in position and shifting of the weight of his body, and he may also use his voice. These may all be called 'natural aids', but there are other 'artificial aids', such as whips, spurs and martingales, which are used to help the legs and hands as means of control and correction.

Legs and hands

Legs come first as they are the rider's most important way of communicating with his horse. They govern the movements of the animal's hindquarters and – since these are what propel the horse – the rider's legs also govern the amount, and to some extent the direction, of the impulsion.

The hands, by means of the reins, act on the horse's mouth and so control his head, neck and shoulders (the 'forehand'). Thus the hands control and guide the horse's forward movement, the legs the expression of the impulsion from behind, and between them the legs and hands can be imagined as forming a sort of tube through which the horse moves.

The voice

As a means of conveying orders to the horse, at least while riding, the voice is not greatly used. Though 'Whoa' and 'Gee-up' and that odd clucking sound are not normally used, the voice is useful in soothing and reassuring the horse. Many riders would benefit from using more often a word such as 'Steady' in a quiet voice, particularly when horses are frightened or excited by a strange sight. At such a time it is all too easy for the horse, with dead silence from his rider, to become 'out of sympathy' with him and act as his own instincts dictate. If this is accompanied, as it so often is, by a feverish shortening of the reins and a tight hold on his head the difficulty is only aggravated.

Naturally enough, all animals are more sensitive to the tone of the voice than to the actual words used, which is why I constantly stress the need for quietness and calmness. Watch a good horseman (or woman) handle horses, and notice how quietly everything is done and how words to the animals are little more than whispers, but – as shown by the flick of an ear – clearly audible to them.

On the other hand, of course, horses are creatures of habit with good memories and do in time come to recognize certain words which they associate with actions required of them. Frequently, for example, the instructor gives the order 'Trot' and sees his pupils' horses obeying before their riders are able to give the necessary aid. This is obviously unfortunate for the rider, being unprepared, is left behind and in any case if the horse does it all the passenger learns nothing.

The body

With regard to changing your position or shifting your weight as part of the instructions to the horse when riding, the way to use this aid can only be explained fully in relation to the various paces and movements. The principle is that by slightly altering the point through which your weight acts in the saddle you change the horse's balance, making him respond in a certain way. By leaning forward or backwards the weight on the forehand or on the hindquarters is correspondingly increased; similarly, leaning slightly to one side increases the weight on that side.

The expert

Perfection in the application of the aids is seen in advanced dressage and Haute Ecole. Here the signals are scarcely perceptible, though the horse's every movement, almost his every breath, is governed by his rider. Such suppleness, balance and obedience in a horse requires years of skilled training, but it shows what can be done.

At whatever stage of proficiency are horse and rider the same qualities of quietness, unobtrusiveness and decision are necessary in the application of the aids. Decision and determination are important, for your horse should not treat you as a mere passenger – he will all too soon come to accept the idea that he knows better than you do: even if he does, it is unwise to let him think so. It is not necessary to be always nagging and worrying at the horse, nor to bully him, but just to keep in touch and be prepared to check instantly any tendency towards his going his own sweet way.

The horse's attention

Before the horse is asked to carry out any order he must be made ready and attentive, rather than being allowed to move at ease. Before an aid is given the horse the rider closes both legs very lightly and sits a little more down in the saddle. This happens a fraction of a second before the feel on the horse's mouth is very slightly increased, just enough to make him realize that something is going to happen. In response to this combination of strengthened driving force from the legs and very light restraint from the rider's hand a trained horse should gather himself together, his hind legs becoming more active and his jaw more relaxed so that he is ready to respond at once to his rider's next request.

This extra attentiveness is sometimes called 'collecting the horse', though true collection is seldom seen except in the carefully and skilfully trained animal. 'Collection' implies that the horse puts more energy into his movements, using his hind legs to give more drive, but remains light and responsive to his rider's hands. It is easy to give oneself, and perhaps some onlookers, the impression of collection by pulling at the horse's head so that he arches his neck and moves more slowly. This is wrong, however, for unless there is sufficient 'push' from the rider's seat and legs there will not be the necessary activation of the horse's back end and he will just become stiff.

'Attentiveness' better describes the mental and physical attitude we want from our horse before we ask him to do something.

8

Dismounting

It is usual in books on riding to include instruction in mounting and dismounting in the same chapter, but I have departed from the accepted system as it seems more logical to describe the procedures in their natural order, as they occur in the stages of practical instruction.

The first lesson in a serious course of instruction can be expected to cover no more than has been described so far in this book – including of course this chapter. Probably no more than half an hour will be spent actually in the saddle during your first riding lesson, and it is foolish to spend longer, for muscles are brought into unaccustomed use and they require time to develop. Also, each stage of learning to ride should be thoroughly grasped before you move on to the next, and this foundation work in particular should not be hurried.

Excluding the involuntary method, there are four acceptable ways of dismounting. They are: (1) the roll; (2) the vault; (3) the method using the stirrups; and (4) what might be called the 'side' method.

The roll

This is the easiest, the safest and probably the most usual way of dismounting and the one which the novice rider is strongly recommended to adopt.

The rider quits both stirrups, places his hands on the horse's shoulders with the arms straight, leans forward over the animal's neck and, throwing the right leg up and over the saddle, jumps to the ground, landing on his toes in line with the horse's forelegs.

The vault

By this method the rider frees both feet from the stirrups and, placing both hands on the pommel of the saddle, throws both legs up and back so that they are together horizontally above the saddle. He then swings his legs forward to the nearside and lands, as before, in line with the horse's forefeet. His right hand, of course, retains its hold on the reins. This method can be used when the horse is moving, though care must be taken to be ready to run on a pace or two with the horse.

With stirrups

This method is merely a reversal of mounting with stirrups. The rider takes the reins in his left hand with sufficient feeling to prevent the horse's moving forward. He takes his right foot from the stirrup, leans forward supporting his weight with both hands on the pommel and passes his right leg backwards over the saddle to the ground, taking the right hand from the saddle as the toe comes to the ground. He is now in a similar position to one in the first stages of mounting – facing towards the horse's hindquarters, with the left foot in the stirrup.

With a tall horse or a short rider there may be some difficulty in freeing the left foot from the stirrup, which is one reason why this method of dismounting is not to be recommended. Some horsemen get over the difficulty by quitting the left stirrup as the right foot reaches the left, and jumping to the ground from there, and this has the advantage of reducing the risk of your foot being caught in the iron should the horse move away. Even so, using the stirrup to dismount always carries with it this risk of being dragged, your foot caught in the stirrup and the horse jumping sideways away from this frightening bundle attached to his saddle, and for that reason alone this method is not recommended.

The side

This way of dismounting is not advised either, and anyway it should only be attempted on a horse that is known to be amenable to it; some horses object strongly, and react accordingly.

To dismount this way the rider quits both stirrups and, with the reins in the left hand, crooks his right leg forward over the saddle, at the same time passing the reins to his right hand, and slides to the ground. The most serious danger here is that the rider may over-balance backwards and fall to the ground head first should the horse move unexpectedly.

Whichever way you choose to dismount, take care to retain the reins – this includes the involuntary method too, if you can!

After dismounting, unless you intend re-mounting almost immediately, it is the practice to 'run the irons up', that is to say, slide the stirrup irons up the underneath part of the leathers till they reach the bar and then secure them by passing the loop of the leather through the iron. This prevents the stirrups banging and flapping about as the horse moves and makes it easier to remove the saddle; it also avoids any such accident as the horse catching a hind foot in one of the irons (cases have been known where horses have actually done this while attempting to scratch an ear with a hind hoof).

It is also customary to loosen the horse's girth a few holes when you dismount, and to pass the reins over his head (being careful not to frighten him) to make it easier to hold or lead him. Once you have dismounted remember that the horse must always be held with a bridle or headcollar until he is safely tied up or delivered back to his stable or field. A loose horse will often panic and gallop blindly, and with modern traffic density this could well be disastrous should he escape on to a road.

9

Walk, Turns, Halt and Rein Back

At long last you can begin to put into practice what you have been learning in the first stages of your lesson.

Before expecting the horse to carry out any movements you will remember that he must be ready and attentive. So, once mounted and settled in the saddle, you apply very gentle pressure with your legs and almost at the same time an even feel on both reins. The horse is prepared to move forward, and to make him do so you ease the feel of your fingers on the reins, maintaining the pressure with your legs.

But what if he just goes backwards? What's wrong? Well, in your anxiety you have kept up, and even exaggerated, your feel on his mouth. Relax your hand, then, and you will find that the horse moves forward; as soon as he is walking out freely you can relax the pressure of your legs against his sides, too. As the horse walks you will notice that he does not keep his head stiff and still but moves it a little in time with his stride. You will have to allow for this by the elasticity of your feel on the reins, though there is no need for your hand actually to move to and fro.

With insufficient feeling on his mouth the horse will carry his head low and his walk will consequently be slovenly; on the other hand, with too strong a feel, his step will be shortened. So watch this point and also remember to apply just sufficient propulsion by means of your legs to keep him walking out – not too much or he will break into a trot.

At the walk you will hear four distinct beats as the hoofs

come to the ground: first, the off-forefoot, second the near hind, third the near fore and fourth the off-hind. When the horse is properly 'supported' by the rider these beats will be regular.

Turns

As soon as you are comfortable at the walk and can keep the horse walking out evenly, you should practise making him change direction. The correct method of turning when the horse is in motion is – as ever – the one where he makes full use of his hindquarters to propel him in the new direction. The horse naturally tends to pivot round his centre but in turning this way he makes it harder for himself because he makes no allowance for his rider's weight and wastes some of the propulsive potential of his back legs.

Let us try to turn to the right, using the three 'aids', reins, legs and body. With the horse moving forward evenly and attentively the forehand (head, neck and shoulders, you will remember) is led round by the right rein, with the left rein pressed lightly against the horse's neck. At the same time your left leg is closed to the horse's side behind the girth to prevent his hindquarters' swinging out to the left, and your body is leaned very slightly back and to the right. Most important, the rider's right leg is pressed against the horse on the girth to create the necessary impulsion. In this turn to the right the animal's off-hindleg is the pivot.

A few points to be borne in mind are that the pressure on the right rein is outward, not directly backward, and that the lean of the body is very slight – in fact little more than a trifling shift of the weight, imperceptible to the onlooker.

The principle is to lead with the inside rein (the one on the side to which you wish to turn), supported by the opposite, or outside, rein and leg, and the weight of the body shifted slightly inwards and back, combined with drive from your inside leg. This is an example of the use of 'diagonal' aids – inside rein, outside leg – for the horse actually moves round part of a circle and should bend the whole length of his spine into an arc as he makes the turn.

Apply these aids until the horse has turned in the direction in which you wish to go, then allow his head to straighten by restoring the reins to the normal position, relaxing the pressure on your outside leg and bringing your weight once more to the centre of the saddle. Keep the horse moving ahead at the same even pace.

I have described a turn carried out with the reins held in two hands with the inside rein used directly. Riding with one hand, typically in the Western style of riding, you can use 'indirect reining', where you do not lead the forehand round with the inside rein but turn the horse by pressure against his neck with the outside rein supported by the outside leg and assisted by your weight being brought towards the rear and the inside: these may be called 'lateral' aids (outside rein and outside leg). The rein-hand moves forward as well as sideways in this neck-reining.

Turn on the haunches

The ultimate utilization of the horse's hindlegs in turning is seen in the formal turn on the haunches. Easiest from the halt, but done by a trained horse from any pace, the horse turns with almost his and his rider's entire weight borne by his hindquarters.

The opposite of this movement is the turn on forehand, where the horse uses his front legs as a pivot and swings his hindquarters round them. This movement is performed only from the halt, and to instruct the horse to do it the rider feels the rein on the side opposite to that towards which it is desired that the horse should swing his hindquarters, say the left. The other rein is also felt, less strongly but sufficiently to prevent the horse's moving forward, and the left leg is applied some 4 inches behind the girth so that the animal's hindquarters are pushed round to the right, away from the leg. The turn on the forehand is a most useful exercise for both horse and rider, and has practical use in manoeuvring the horse in order to open a gate while mounted.

Halt

To bring the horse to a halt, both the rider's legs are closed gently against the saddle and the feel on both reins is increased evenly; at the same time the weight of the body is brought very slightly back in the saddle. The horse should come to the halt properly balanced and standing squarely; as soon as he responds to your aids by stopping, relax them so that you are sitting easily.

Rein back

The horse should rein back, that is step backwards, slowly and regularly, and moving in a straight line. In walking backwards he should actually move his feet two and two, the near-fore and off-hind (left diagonal) and then the off-fore and near-hind (right diagonal) so that the rein back is in two time.

To make the horse rein back he is first made attentive. Close your legs lightly as you would to make him walk forward, but instead of giving with your hands, keep them steady, but sympathetic. As you resist the horse's tendency to move on, lean forward slightly yourself. The hand thus acts as a barrier, the horse wanting to move on finds that he can't, so he naturally steps back. The horse should never be hauled back by the reins alone, and only a few steps should be taken at a time, the rider relaxing hands and legs as the horse complies with his wishes. Many horses, it will be found, are trained to respond to the command 'Back' given with the appropriate aids.

10

The Trot

The trot, the next pace after the walk, is often difficult for the beginner to master. Practice in trotting should be carried out in easy stages, a few minutes at a time, otherwise stiffness and soreness may be experienced as a result.

The aids to make the horse break into a trot are similar to those used to make him walk on, that is to say with the horse walking out attentively, close both your legs to his sides just behind the girth and ease both reins slightly. As soon as he breaks into a trot of the required speed, the pressure of the legs may be relaxed, but the necessary light feel on the reins should be maintained.

Your aim is to rise at the trot and so avoid that tiring bumping, but, before attempting to rise, I am afraid you will have to bump along for a bit to get the feel of things. To ask you to do this for more than a very short time, though, would be unkind to both you and the horse; the horse's lot is made more pleasant if you hang on to a neckstrap or the pommel of the saddle, rather than the reins, until you begin to feel reasonably secure.

The trot is a two-time gait, the horse springing from one diagonal to the other (which is why you tend to be thrown out of the saddle uncomfortably at each stride). The order in which the horse's feet hit the ground is near-fore and off-hind together, then off-fore and near-hind. The normal speed of the trot is some 8 miles per hour, so it is a useful gait when you actually want to get somewhere.

When the rider bumps he comes into the saddle in time with each diagonal's hitting the ground – tiring for both man and horse. By 'rising' to the trot the rider times the rise and fall of his body so that he sits in the saddle as one diagonal touches the ground. As the feet of that diagonal (off-fore and near-hind if it is the right diagonal) are in the air making a stride forward the rider's seat is out of the saddle.

Learning to 'rise' to the trot is thus a knack of timing; for a while it seems impossible that you will ever learn it, but once it is mastered you do it quite automatically and you find yourself wondering why on earth you found learning to 'rise' so difficult. The points to remember in the rising trot are that the knees should be kept on the saddle and that the lower legs should keep their position, slightly back, with the stirrup leathers taut. With your heels sunk, keep the pressure on the stirrup irons with the ball of your foot. No exertion is needed, and your body should be supple from the hips, with the stomach kept in. You may be told to 'rise over your hands'. Exactly what is meant by this may not be very clear to you. If we say the body will be leaning forward very slightly and the hands will be steady in their usual position at about waist level it may make the instruction more understandable. Take care not to bob your hands up and down with the movements of your body, for this is quite a common fault, particularly when the elbows and forearms are stiffened up. Your hands and arms must remain quite independent of the movements of the rest of your body.

When you first try rising at the trot you will notice that the horse's head is held higher and closer to his body than at the walk, so that the reins will have to be shortened a little before you give the aid to 'trot on'. At a properly balanced trot the horse keeps his head fairly still but, just the same, the rider's hands and arms will be ready to respond to give to any movement of it. Keep your lower legs steady – at first there is always a tendency to let your legs move – and try to rise from your knees, rather than by placing your whole weight on the stirrups. It is not necessary to push yourself up, and doing so makes for stiffness of the whole body. Are your neck muscles relaxed? If not it is obvious that you are holding yourself stiffly and exerting yourself unnecessarily.

FIG. 5. THE TROT

An illustration of the pace of two time on alternate diagonals, that is: Near fore and off hind, followed by off fore and near hind. This explains the 'bumping' sensation of the trot and the reason for 'rising' to ease both horse and rider. Note the position of the hands, and that the body leans forward only very slightly without any hunching of the shoulders or crouching. There must be no stiffness and no exertion; the lower legs are steady and without grip, and the knees act as hinges and provide any grip necessary. The feet are in the normal position, with sufficient pressure to keep the stirrup irons steady and the leathers taut.

Let your knees act as hinges and you will find that the horse will do the rest.

As you progress, you will notice that your seat does not come into the saddle with a bump, but lightly and gently. Personally, I hate to see a horse's back sag in the middle every time a heavy rider hits the saddle with a thump, it reminds one of a comic cartoon, as does the other common mistake, easy to make at first, where the rider sticks out his toes and elbows like wings and flippers.

If the rider's toes are turned out, not only are the heels brought into the horse's sides, but the backs of the calves come against the saddle and consequently the knees lose contact. Another fault which is not uncommon is to lift the elbows away from the sides and hunch the shoulders in an attempt to lift the body.

Changing diagonals

The rider's weight can be in the saddle either when the horse's left diagonal or when his right diagonal is on the ground. To keep the horse even and to ease him during a long period of trotting the rider should change diagonals at intervals. This is done simply by sitting for one or three strides – that is one or three 'bumps'. Most horses have one diagonal which they prefer and which is stronger than the other so that you may find that you are rather thrown about when you come to sit on the less favoured diagonal. Even so, you should persevere, for in school work the rider should sit as the inside hind leg (that is on the left diagonal on a right-handed circle, and *vice versa*) hits the ground.

The sitting trot

The rider should be capable of sitting still in the saddle as the horse trots, but this is considerably harder to master than the rising trot and requires much more suppleness, and better balance and sympathy with the horse's movement. Some instructors maintain that trotting without stirrups will teach a rider to sit deeper in the saddle; this may be true of the reasonably competent rider, but for the novice the exercise is an uncomfortable one, with more bumping about than sitting, and to be tackled for short periods only, if at all.

On the other hand, from the beginning the learner rider should attempt to sit down at the trot when making turns, or asking the horse to change pace. At first try it for a few strides only and with the horse going at a slow trot; with your stirrups the right length and your heels pressed well down you will find that it is not too difficult to sit still.

The aids for turning at the trot are the same as for turns at any other gait, though impulsion is maintained better if the rider sits down and steadies the horse a little before the turn.

Slowing down and stopping

To slow the horse to a walk the rider sits down in the saddle, closes both legs on the horse's sides, brings his weight back in the saddle and increases the feeling on the reins. When he has come to a walk the aids are relaxed and sufficient rein given to permit normal head-carriage. To halt from the walk similar aids are used and maintained until the horse stops and stands correctly balanced.

As far as possible trotting should be confined to soft going, and is really best avoided on made-up roads because of the jarring of the animal's legs which results from the constant trotting on a hard surface with the weight of a rider; there is also the likelihood of slipping on modern tarmac. When a horse is trotted on the road he should be made to do so steadily and rhythmically, avoiding the 'butcher boy trot' – traditionally flat out as the lad drove his master's horse home at the end of the day.

11

The Canter and Gallop

The canter is the next fastest pace after the trot and is one that should only be used on softish ground, never on the road, and in speed should not exceed nine or ten miles an hour.

Before going into the explanation of the canter let us first get the feel of it for a few minutes. So, while at the trot, sit down in the saddle and squeeze with the legs, at the same time maintaining light contact with the horse's mouth.

The point that will be noticed immediately in the first try-out of the canter is the tendency for the rider to bump in the saddle or, as someone once said, 'It is very easy to rise at the canter!'

But at the canter the rider should sit still in the saddle, neither deliberately rising nor bumping. To do this he must sit well down and, above all, relax. The body must not be allowed to slouch but be kept upright with shoulders back and square; if you crouch forward it is very hard to avoid bumping and your lower legs will tend to move back behind the perpendicular so that you cannot use them effectively and will therefore have less control over the horse. On the other hand, if the body is leaned back, the lower leg is pushed forward and the rider's weight put on the horse's loins.

With the legs in the correct position, maintain just sufficient pressure on the stirrup irons to retain them – too much pressure will cause stiffness and bumping. The elbows should be relaxed too but they should be still – there is often a tendency to let them flap about in a most unbecoming manner.

Remembering these points, you should try another short

canter, driving the seat down and forward into the saddle, and at the same time keeping your body supple. Another point that you will notice is that the forward and backward movement of the horse's head is more marked than at the trot, and therefore you must be prepared to 'give' to him still more from the elbows and shoulders as well as wrists and fingers. Some practice will be required before you master the canter and are able to sit down firmly and quietly in the saddle, making the horse keep up a steady, rhythmic gait.

The canter is a 'three-time gait'. With the 'near-fore leading', the order in which the horse's feet come to the ground is: off-hind, then the right diagonal (off-fore and near-hind simultaneously), and the near-fore last. The near-fore leg is advanced more than the off, which is why the horse would be said to be 'leading with his near-fore'. You will also notice that the near-hind seems to lead the off-hind. The pattern is reversed if the horse canters with the 'off-fore leading'. Then the sequence of feet coming to the ground in each stride is: near-hind, then the left diagonal together and, last, the off-fore.

On a circle or turn, the horse should always lead with the inside leg; that is the left lead for a left turn or circle to the left, and right lead for right turns or circles. Occasionally a horse seems to get his legs working in the wrong sequence, so that he is 'leading' with, say, the off-fore and the near-hind, or vice versa. This is called a 'disunited' canter, and makes for a very bumpy and uncomfortable ride, besides unbalancing the horse.

If you wish the horse to strike off into a canter with off-fore and off-hind leading, first get him going at a steady trot on a right hand circle. Sit down for a few strides, and make sure he is attentive before you apply the necessary aids. These are to lean your body very slightly back and to the inside of the circle, at the same time turning the horse's head slightly to the right, closing both legs on the saddle with the left a little further back than the right. Thus the stronger leg aid is applied on the side of the first of the horse's legs to make a canter stride – the near-hind in this case.

When the horse is cantering united and on the correct leg his head is straightened up to the direction in which he is moving. To canter with the other leg leading, that is near-fore and hind leading, simply reverse the aids, giving more pressure with the right leg and a stronger feel with the left rein. After a little practice you will find that you can feel with which leg the horse is leading at the canter and you will not need to peer down over his shoulder to find out.

Turning

Turns at the canter should not be too sharp and it is particularly important that the horse should be properly steadied and cantering united. It is difficult for him to turn in a direction away from the leading leg, and if he is made to do so fast there is the risk that he could cross his legs and fall over!

The aids for turning at the canter are similar to those for turns at other paces. The horse's hindlegs must be brought under him and prevented from flying out by pressure from the rider's outward leg, and the outside rein can be used to support the inside or direct rein.

Slowing down and stopping

The aids are, of course, the same as for other paces, but care should be taken not to attempt to pull up too sharply. This is an occasion where the voice may be used with advantage to help slow the horse down steadily, giving him warning of what is required. Pulling up abruptly on the haunches from a fast pace looks very fine and dashing in the cowboy film or on the polo ground, but cutting horses and polo ponies are trained for this sort of thing. Attempting such sudden stops on the ordinary riding horse usually results in a lot of hauling on his mouth and – to say the least – loss of harmony between horse and rider.

The aid for transition from canter to trot consists of the rider's giving a gentle feel on the reins, rather stronger on the side opposite to that of the horse's leading leg, that is –

on a circle – on the outside rein. As soon as the horse complies the hand relaxes to him in reward.

THE GALLOP

At no pace should you let the horse travel faster than you wish, but I would particularly impress on the beginner the need to keep back to a properly controlled speed at the gallop and to retain contact with the horse's mouth. That

FIG. 6. THE SLOW GALLOP

The horse must be under perfect control, so that he is instantly responsive to the aids. Note that there is little difference between the rider's position at this and her position when the horse is standing or walking. She sits close in the saddle, and, being balanced, needs to exert the minimum of grip – this being with the knees and thighs only, leaving the lower legs free to apply their aids when necessary. The hands are kept low, with only sufficient feeling on the horse's mouth to retain control.

may sound like an unnecessary piece of advice but it is surprising how many novices think that at the gallop they just career along with reins flapping and all idea of control and feeling blowing away behind them with their hats. The horse must still be under your command, responsive and ready instantly to slow down smoothly and quietly without any fighting or head-tossing.

Earlier in this book mention was made of the horse's strong instinct for self-preservation. In the natural state he takes refuge from danger in flight, so to allow him to have his head and gallop madly, without communication with his rider, arouses ancestral, wild-horse feelings in him.

There are two alternative positions which may be adopted for the gallop.

In the first, which is used in the ordinary way when the pace is not fast or the horse needs a certain amount of encouragement, the rider sits down close in the saddle, gripping with knees and thighs. This grip should not be too tight, or as much as will distress the horse, as it is possible for a very muscular rider to do.

The hands should be kept low, with sufficient feeling on the reins to keep perfect control of the horse; this feeling should, even so, be light and sensitive, as pulling on the horse's mouth will only encourage him to fight against the bit.

In the alternative – the forward seat – which is adopted at a fast pace or with an animal that gallops freely without any driving – the rider adopts a more forward position, crouching his body and raising his weight from the saddle on his knees, thighs and stirrups. In order to keep a continuous light feel on the horse's mouth the reins have to be shortened, but they should never be used by the rider for support. The position is useful when galloping over rough ground, or for long periods, which are likely to tire the horse.

Turning, slowing down and stopping

These are carried out as at other gaits, but obviously at this faster pace more care must be taken and more time allowed.

Fig. 7. THE FAST GALLOP

Here is shown the crouched position at a fast gallop. The rider's
weight is thrown forward and taken on his knees and stirrups,
lifting his body clear of the seat of the saddle and offering the least
interference to the stride and thrust of the horse's hindlegs. In this
racing gallop it is necessary, of course, to use a much shorter
rein than at a slow pace in order to retain the correct feeling of the
horse's mouth, and the whole of the arms must be prepared to give
to the movements of his head.

In turning, a larger sweep needs to be taken than at the
canter and slowing down should be gradual and the necessary distance judged and allowed for stopping completely.
With regard to halting suddenly, I would say again that in
ordinary everyday riding there really is no justification for
pulling the horse about in this manner; in an emergency a
rapid stop can be achieved by very strong application of the
normal aids for reduction of pace.

12

Jumping

Before undertaking jumping lessons it is essential that you should have a firm, balanced and independent seat and be able to control your horse really well. Jumping does help to confirm a good seat, as well as being fun in itself, but good progress should have been made first.

There is nothing difficult or at all frightening about jumping, particularly as at the beginning no very large obstacles will be placed in your path. In fact, the best way to start is by attempting only very low fences, over which the horse would have no difficulty in stepping at a walk.

Reduced to its simplest terms, you know that as the horse jumps he raises his forequarters and propels his whole body upwards and forward, the power being supplied by the hind legs' straightening and thrusting. In landing the forefeet touch the ground first, the hindlegs following almost immediately. When the horse pops over a small obstacle all this happens so quickly that it is hard to break down the action of jumping into its component parts.

Occasionally a horse will tend to 'cat-jump', and land with all four feet touching the ground at the same moment. Here considerable shock is felt by horse and rider, particularly as such ungainly leaps are often made by a reluctant animal that approaches the fence slowly and only under duress.

So much, very briefly, for the horse. Now what of the rider?

I have already said that for your first jumping lessons you should make a modest start; this is important so that you do not lose confidence. No one can be expected to learn to jump well and ride fluently over fences if he fears a fall, nor will a nervous horse perform well.

Many instructors choose to teach both horses and riders (though not together – novice horse and learner rider is a very bad combination) to jump by asking them to tackle sequences of poles lying on the ground, which the horse walks and trots over. Later, the poles may be raised a few inches so that the horse makes rather more effort to step over them, though he does not have to actually jump. The great value of these 'cavaletti' to the rider are that they enable him to practise a correct jumping position.

For jumping the rider takes his weight out of the saddle, bearing it on knees, thighs and stirrups (never hands) as described for the 'forward' seat at the gallop. Balance plays a more important part in keeping the rider in the saddle than does grip, the knees being pressed against the saddle only firmly enough to keep them in their place and give assistance as required.

The lower leg should remain in its normal position, neither thrust forward nor drawn back; it may be found easier to maintain a correct position over fences if the stirrup leathers are shortened by one or two holes.

The rider's hands should remain independent of the rest of his body, though during early attempts at jumping and negotiating cavaletti this may be found very difficult, and a neckstrap which you can catch hold of will save your jerking the horse in the mouth accidentally. A light and constant feel, sympathetic to the movements of his head, should be kept on the horse's mouth, and that straight line from elbow to bit maintained.

It is well to remember that, in jumping, the horse's head and neck will be stretched forward considerably as he makes his effort and your hands must be prepared for more 'give' than would be required while riding on the flat, if you are not to interfere with his head yet retain contact. The neckstrap will be found very useful if you feel insecure and that you are going to be 'left behind' as the horse stretches out. Failing a neckstrap, hang on to the pommel of the saddle, or even a handful of mane, to avoid the unforgivable crime of jabbing the horse in the mouth, or landing on his back with a great thump. Rather than interfere with the horse's head, if you feel that you are unavoidably going to be rather left behind, try to let the reins slip through your fingers so that the horse's head is left free.

As the horse approaches a fence the rider should be sitting quietly in the saddle, ready and able to push the horse on with legs and seat should he show any reluctance to jump. By sitting in the saddle the rider is also in a more secure position should the horse try any evasion, like refusing or running out to one side.

As the horse takes off the rider leans his body forward, naturally but without exaggeration, and his seat comes out of the saddle. Over the fence the rider is in the forward position, his hands low to allow for the horse's dropping his head and stretching his neck, as described already. Soon after landing over the fence the rider assumes again the position, either 'forward' with seat just out of the saddle, or 'upright', sitting in the saddle, suitable for the pace at which the horse is going.

Having reached the stage where cavaletti and small jumps can be taken correctly and with perfect confidence you can pass on to larger obstacles, perhaps of some two foot six inches high.

We now have to begin to think of the approach to the fence and the timing of the horse's leap. Over low fences the whole business can safely be left to the sensible and experienced horse, who will shorten or lengthen his last few strides so that he 'meets the fence right'. This means that he arrives at a take-off point which is about five or six feet from a two foot six inches jump – the bigger the jump the further away from it must be the take-off point – and at take-off the horse is balanced, with his hind legs well under his body so that he can make his spring.

Badly timed interference from the rider during the approach to a fence may well unbalance the horse and bring him to the obstacle 'all wrong'. And certainly I say leave it

Fig. 8. THE TAKE-OFF

The rider has lifted his weight from the horse's back and has taken
it on his knees and stirrups. In this position his centre of gravity is
on a line passing through the stirrups. The horse's loins are free
from weight and his head and neck have freedom of movement,
whilst the rider retains perfect control throughout the jump.

to the horse in a case where a mistake has been made over a
tricky place and realized, possibly, when it is too late for the
rider to do anything about it. In such instances many horses
have a happy knack of righting themselves cleverly if they
are allowed perfect freedom to do so.

Fig. 9. LANDING

On landing, the rider's body resumes the normal upright position –
this is the position to be aimed at throughout the jump by allowing
the trunk to sway slightly backwards with the horse's movement
after the take-off. There must be a light feeling of the mouth all the
time, to retain control, which argues considerable 'give' right from
the shoulders according to the height of the jump, but on no
account should the horse's balance be upset by a dead pull or by
jabbing. Beginners would be wise to make use of a neck strap or
even the pommel of the saddle to keep their balance and to avoid
interfering with the mouth. Perhaps a better method, in the early
lessons, is for them to drop the reins entirely until they have
acquired perfect balance. The drawing shows clearly how for a
moment on landing the horse bears all the weight on one foreleg,
which indicates the strain to which it may be subjected.

On the other hand, wise interference from the rider may be necessary where, for example, a horse is tending to approach a fence too fast, so that he can only adjust his stride by shortening it and in slowing down to do this he loses valuable momentum. Over large and difficult fences the take-off point becomes more critical, so that half a stride too near or too far out make the difference between clearing the fence or ploughing through it. The rider's assistance to the horse in judging his take-off point and bringing him to it then becomes important, particularly so, for example, in show jumping where it is of paramount importance that the horse should jump cleanly.

A horse should be moving steadily and attentively as he approaches a fence, with his hind legs well under him and very active. Facing the fence squarely, within three strides of the point from which it is estimated the actual leap should be made, the speed is slightly increased as the horse is pushed on. The third stride should bring you to the correct take-off area and here, with an equal pressure with both legs, you send him up and over.

With practice it is quite easy to judge and time the approach and take-off correctly.

In leaping an obstacle such as stream or ditch where there is no height, only width, it should be remembered that the horse's spine will still form an arc as he jumps, though it will be a lower, rather flatter one than over an upright fence. It is this perfect arc, or 'bascule', formed by the horse's head and neck and his rounded back that is so important if a horse is to perform really well over large jumps.

13

Beyond the First Stages . . .

Jumping a horse is fun, but be careful not to sicken the horse by asking him to go over the same obstacle time and time again. You can make the jumping more interesting, both for you and for your mount, by varying the fences, and by including some ground work, in the form of elementary dressage, which will make the horse more supple and obedient.

You may decide that you enjoy jumping so much that you want to take the first steps towards emulating the show-jumping stars by competing in the jumping competitions at local horse shows. But there is more to competitive riding than just show-jumping, where the relatively small arena, the painted fences, and the standardized format impose a certain, set, style of riding and training the horse.

'Combined Training', for instance, is a mixture of dressage and jumping, and is becoming increasingly popular; it ranges from the severe test of the Three-Day-Event to simple competitions entailing an elementary dressage test and a straightforward jumping course.

The basis of the Three-Day-Event is the cross-country Speed and Endurance Test, performed on the second day. In this, competitors have to gallop over about four miles of a steeplechase course at racing pace, and another five miles over a course of large, solid, natural fences; the rest of the twenty odd miles of the Speed and Endurance Phase is covered at brisk hacking pace. On the day after this, the third day, there is a show-jumping phase, in which horse and rider show that they have recovered from the exertions of the day before.

On the first day of the Three-Day-Event the rider has to perform a dressage test to show that the horse is supple, balanced and obedient in these precise movements, even though he is ready to really gallop on and tackle big fences the next day. The dressage is a telling part of the competition, and so it should be, for this basic schooling of the horse to obey his rider's instructions, and to carry himself correctly, is essential for any riding horse, an eventer or show-jumper as much as any other.

Though 'dressage' sounds very grand, the word's derivation implies only correctness of placing and precision, in this case of the horse. The horse's training, and his rider's ability, to perform certain movements is all that is called for in the dressage test, which is carried out in a marked out arena. Movements range from ordinary walking, trotting and cantering around the rectangular arena, with a halt and changes of direction, to the complex work, such as that 'on two tracks' – that is, with the horse moving not in a straight line forward but at an angle to the direction in which he is facing – of the more senior tests.

This same dressage 'arena' is basically the same rectangular riding school that is used for teaching riding, with set points marked with letters. Rectangular, and usually about 40 metres long by 20 wide, it permits the rider to describe circles, and figures of eight, and to ride across diagonal and centre lines – and, simple though riding in a straight line may seem at first glance, it is much harder to keep a horse really straight, along the whole length of his body, than you would think.

Elementary dressage work will require no more outlandish movements than the ordinary walk, trot and canter, simple transitions from one gait to another, and changes of direction. At the other end of the scale, the horse trained by an expert rider to advanced standard will be capable of such difficult movements as the pirouette or *piaffé* (trot on the spot). Dressage for the average rider and horse is unlikely to progress beyond just making the horse reasonably obedient and pleasant to ride; this training will continue, however, whenever you ride the horse, whether in a marked arena or just along the road.

You will find that your dressage training is applied at all sorts of unexpected times, too. If you decide to compete at a local gymkhana (which is a selection of races, such as 'Ride and Run', or a 'Sack Race', where competitors ride to a sack and then run in the sack, leading their ponies) you may find yourself in a 'Bending Race'. In this you have to weave in and out of a line of about half a dozen posts placed about eight metres apart. And what are you doing, but a series of half circles, with a change of direction, and of leading leg if you are cantering, between each?

You may decide that competitive riding is not in your line, and that once you are reasonably proficient on a horse, you would prefer to ride for no other reason than the pleasure of being on a horse. And what better reason could there be? You will find hacking delightful and you may decide to investigate pony trekking as a pastime to be enjoyed in this country or abroad. In Britain there are a number of long distance bridlepaths, often passing through magnificent country, and these offer a very good opportunity to 'get away from it all'.

Or you may come to the conclusion that some of everything will give you most enjoyment from your riding; a few local horse shows and hunter trials (jumping natural fences across country), a few days' hunting in winter, the occasional day-ride in summer, regular hacking and some dressage and jumping in the school now and again.

Whatever you choose to do, or you find yourself doing, in the riding line, don't forget that there are a number of societies for people with similar interests in horses. For young people there is the Pony Club, a countrywide organization, which will give much help and encouragement. The Pony Club is affiliated to the British Horse Society, a large national organization, and to the B.H.S. are also affiliated a number of local riding clubs which generally cater for adults as well as, possibly, young riders. There are, of course, a number of other societies and clubs for those interested in horses and riding, and most will welcome new members, whatever their standard of accomplishment in the saddle.

14

When the Horse 'Plays Up'

To return to a more mundane aspect of riding, we have to face the fact that our horses do sometimes misbehave. Here are some suggestions about how to deal with a few of the more common problems.

Mounting a restive horse

Many horses develop the disconcerting habit of walking off while being mounted, which is often due to their having received a dig in the ribs from the toe of the careless rider as he mounts – and can you really blame the horse? To restrict the animal's movement, the off-rein is taken up shorter than the near so that the horse's head is turned slightly to the right and any movement of his body can only bring it closer to the rider. And be sure to push your left toe well down and so avoid digging the horse's side.

With a horse which is fidgety and restive the rider may find that there is no difficulty if the reins are left loose, the horse having been frightened by a jab in the mouth. If this method is unsuccessful, try taking hold of the cheek piece of the bridle with your left hand, so that the horse's head is perforce turned to his left side, and taking up the reins loosely, with your right hand placed well over to the off-side of the pommel when your left foot is in the stirrup; this method is often effective.

Jogging

A bad habit which some horses have, and which is most annoying to the rider, is that of jogging instead of walking properly. This is tiring for both horse and rider and can easily give either saddle sores. The horse may first do it because of pain from badly fitting saddlery or a sore mouth, or because of persistent niggling at the reins by the rider, and it then becomes a habit. Obviously attention should be paid to the animal's harness and the rider's hands, but horses also jog for other reasons, such as freshness or lack of exercise. If so quiet handling and avoiding a constant pull on the reins will generally make them walk out properly.

Stumbling

Some animals are rather prone to stumbling for various reasons, such as lameness, but it is also frequently due to tiredness or careless riding. A horse that is *ridden* and made to go properly and attentively is far less likely to stumble than one which is allowed to amble along anyhow, half-asleep.

Pressure from the rider's legs, pushing the horse into his bridle to keep his head up will lessen the weight on his fore-legs and bring his haunches under him, thus giving him immediate assistance should he stumble. The same applies, incidentally, going downhill.

Shying

Shying is a sudden movement, usually made to one side, arising from instinctive fear of certain objects, or noises, or unusual sights. It is not uncommon for playfulness to be the sole reason. When the horse shies to one side or swings round sharply the rider's retaining his seat depends on his balance and ability to adjust himself instantly to the horse's movement.

The rider's leg should be applied strongly on the side to which the horse attempts to swing and, if he twists first one way and then the other his head should be turned to one side and the rider's opposite leg applied. The pressure of the leg prevents his swinging to that side and he will never swing towards the direction in which his head is turned. Any attempt to back away should be counteracted by pressure from both legs, and possibly a sharp verbal command.

Should the horse, however, turn right round it is better not to try to stop him but instead to circle him completely until he is facing the right way and then apply both legs and, if necessary, the heels.

It sometimes happens that instead of shying aside the horse comes to a standstill and refuses to budge one way or the other. In such a case the remedy is often very simple: do not try to push him on, just let him stand and in a few seconds he will get bored and move on without further difficulty.

The rider should beware of becoming upset and angry himself; quietness, encouragement and a soothing voice will win in most cases. Punishment is very seldom necessary and, if it is, it should always be administered absolutely calmly and with due consideration, in the certain knowledge that the horse is misbehaving through naughtiness and not fear. Great patience is sometimes required to overcome a horse's doubts about an unusual object, and when he shows signs of nervousness it is well to get him up very gently to it and let him satisfy himself by sight and scent that there is no reason for fear.

Finally, it should be remembered that riders are quite often solely to blame for their horses' shying. Approaching something at which they anticipate the animal may shy, many riders promptly shorten up the reins and tighten their grip on the saddle, so communicating nervousness to the horse, who is not slow to sense that something is up and naturally associates it with the object in view and instinctively seeks to avoid it whereas, but for the rider's reactions, he would very likely have passed it without any fuss.

Pulling and bolting

These troubles are attributable to various causes; too often they may be traced to pain from harsh use of the bit or a sore mouth, but are sometimes only due to freshness and excitability. Whatever the reason, the rider should never exert a dead pull on the reins. It is hopeless to lean back and use your weight to pull against the horse for you only numb his mouth and make matters worse. The feeling on the reins should be alternately relaxed and increased. As an adjunct to balance the knees may be tightened against the saddle, but the lower legs should be kept in their normal position and not drawn back or the heels may be brought into the horse's sides and urge him on still more.

Where space is unrestricted the horse may be given his head and allowed to gallop on freely, which often produces better results than fighting him, either because it is unexpected or because the first burst of energy may be worn off and the horse more easily slowed down then. If there is sufficient room, he may be allowed to gallop until he tires, and if he is then made to gallop still more it may be a useful lesson to him.

In England, such ideal riding country is rare, and becoming more so, and for safety's sake a runaway must be brought back to hand quickly. The most practical way of doing this is by circling, the horse being wheeled in diminishing circles beginning with a wide sweep and gradually closing in until the speed is slow enough to permit the rider to regain control. Riding at a steep hill, if there is one convenient, will also slow down the speed sufficiently to allow the rider to bring his horse under proper control again.

In very exceptional circumstances, possibly to avoid a serious accident, the rider may think it necessary to bale out. He will, of course, try to find a soft spot where he can land in comparative comfort and having found one will free both feet from the stirrups, drop the reins and slip quietly from the saddle, taking care to fall relaxed and land or roll clear of the horse's feet. This may occasion the horse some surprise, and sometimes he may stop to look back and satisfy his curiosity, or his hunger, when he can be re-captured. 'Dropping the pilot' should only be resorted to in an exceptional emergency and, luckily, is very seldom necessary. The writer has only once found it necessary to adopt this measure and was then fortunate enough to find a heap of farmyard manure which is recommended as providing a soft, if somewhat perfumed, landing place. At all other times when leaving the saddle suddenly the hold on the reins should be retained, but on this occasion they should be released, to avoid dragging; the serious risks to life and limb (of other people and the horse) of a frightened horse loose in modern traffic should not be taken lightly, though.

So what if the crime is committed on a track or road? Here the rider must make intelligent use of the means at his disposal, such as an opportunity to turn towards a tall hedge or other safe obstruction. If none such presents itself the rider will have to rely on the reins alone, and if all other means fail and as a last resort, 'sawing' may be effective, though it is painful for the horse and unlikely to improve his mouth. It consists of a strong pull, first on one rein then on the other until the horse finally throws his head up and admits he is beaten.

Every effort should be made to keep the horse collected, with his head in a position affording control, otherwise he will get his head and neck out at full stretch and find it easy to pull. Some horses also pull with their heads thrown up in a position which allows the rider little control; for such animals a standing martingale, effectively a strap from girth to noseband, will help to prevent the head from being raised too high.

Frequently it is fear of some unaccustomed sight that causes bolting and in such cases the fear should be overcome to try and prevent repetition of the trouble, the best way being – as with shying – to introduce the horse to the strange object quietly, using a soothing voice.

Rearing

When a horse rears it is most important to slacken the reins, as a strong feeling on them will only lead to bigger and better rearing. Give him 'all the reins' and lean forward, catching hold of a handful of mane if necessary to keep yourself in the saddle. Leaning forward not only helps the horse keep his balance and avoid going over backwards, but also has the effect of pushing him down.

FIG. 10.   REARING

Give him 'all the reins', as a strong feel on his mouth may lead to higher rearing, with the risk of the horse's over-balancing backwards. Lean forward to aid balance and help push the horse down. A tight-standing martingale may help to discourage a confirmed rearer.

Another method of dealing with rearing is to bring the horse's forefeet down by upsetting his balance. With the reins in both hands, his head is bent to one side with the hand held low, the opposite rein being slackened, and the horse is compelled by this means to move one hindleg and

drop his forefeet in order to keep his balance and remain
upright.

An experienced rider capable of keeping a firm, independent, seat may be able to bring the horse round in tight
circles after rearing and then drive him forward. The circling
momentarily confuses the animal, and is very effective both
for this and for some other disobediences.

Kicking and bucking

It is only comparatively seldom that one meets with real
bucking or strenuous high kicking, but even small bucks call
for a firm and independent seat, if the rider is not to be
dislodged. The rider retains his seat and balance by leaning
back slightly, without stiffness, and keeping his legs closed
on the saddle. The horse's head must be kept up and, although the rider's hands should not pull, they should be
firm. If the horse is kept moving he will be less able to con-
tract the muscles used for bucking and kicking, while playing with the bit will tend to take his mind off contemplated
acrobatics.

By the position a horse adopts, humping his back and
often laying back his ears, the intention to kick can often be
anticipated, particularly when it is directed against another
person or animal, and the rider's leg must prevent the
would-be kicker swinging his hindquarters round ready for
action. There is, of course, practically no disturbance of the
rider's seat in the saddle caused by this kicking at a
'target'.

When a horse is known to be a kicker, care should be
taken to keep his heels away from other horses and the tail
should be decorated with a red ribbon as a warning to other
horsemen; but even a red ribbon does not relieve the
kicker's rider of the responsibility of ensuring that his
mount does not hurt other people or animals.

Apart from a firm and balanced seat, quietness is the
quality required in dealing with these various difficulties,
together with ability to act quickly and, if possible, to anticipate and frustrate the horse's intentions. This is not really

thought-reading, since the horse usually gives notice in one way or another of impending playing up or wrong-doing, such as by the laying back of the ears as a preliminary to kicking and, perhaps the most usual and reliable warning of any nonsense, dropping his bit for an instant. Whatever the warning signal, you should be able to recognize it and act upon it without delay.

15

Bits, Bridles and Bridling

The bridle is that portion of the horse's harness which holds the bit in his mouth. Apart from the bit itself, the bridle is made up of four parts which, in the order in which they lie on the horse's head, are as follows.

The noseband, which although usually fitted is not essential, holds itself in position by a strap passing over the horse's poll, fastening by means of a buckle on the near-side. The actual noseband is adjusted and fastened by a buckle under the horse's jaw.

The cheek pieces or cheek straps are attached at one end to the bit by means of buckles, studs or stitching and at the other to the headpiece by buckles.

The headpiece passes over the horse's head, lying on top of the noseband's supporting strap, and is kept in place by the throatlash, which is part of it, fastening round the throat and buckling on the near-side.

The last item is the browband, which crosses the forehead and has a loop at either end, through which passes the supporting strap of the noseband and the bit headstall.

In fitting the bridle, the ordinary Cavesson noseband is so adjusted that it lies two fingers' breadth below the horse's cheekbone and should be loose enough to admit at least two fingers between itself and the jaw. The throatlash should be no tighter than is necessary to prevent the bridle slipping forward over the horse's ears and loose enough to permit the breadth of the hand between the throatlash and the horse's lower jaw. The browband, whose purpose is to keep the bridle from slipping backwards, should not be so tight that it rubs the horse's head or the base of his ears.

Correct bitting – that is to the use of the type of bit best suited to that particular animal – so that he is comfortable yet perfectly under the rider's control – calls for some experience. Horses vary considerably as regards sensitivity of mouth, and a horse unsuitably bitted will not perform to his best advantage. He may even be encouraged to play up because of discomfort in his mouth.

To all intents and purposes there are only three main types of bridle: the snaffle, the double bridle and the pelham, practically all others being variations of these basic patterns.

The snaffle

The snaffle has already been described briefly (Page 31) and all that need be mentioned now are some of the variants, such as the twisted and straight bar snaffles. In the first of these the mouthpiece is jointed as before but is twisted so that there are grooves in the metal, which make it a more severe bit than the plain, smooth model.

In the straight snaffle the mouthpiece is one complete bar of metal and has not the nutcracker effect of the jointed variety, though it does bear directly on the horse's tongue.

A problem with any snaffle bit is that the horse's lips may be pinched at the point where the ring and the mouthpiece meet, and this is particularly nasty when the hole in the mouthpiece has worn and developed a sharp burr. To avoid this the 'egg-butt' snaffle is available, where the mouthpiece is extended to a T-piece at each end, and is jointed through this to the bit ring. Another alternative is the 'Fulmer' pattern cheek snaffle; in this bit the mouthpiece forms a blunt-ended spike at either end, and is jointed to the bit ring beyond the spike. In use it is the smooth right-angle between the cheek or spike and the mouthpiece that comes into contact with the horse's lips. This bit also has the advantage that, when the upper spike is secured to the cheek piece of the bridle, as it always should be, the bit lies very still in the horse's mouth, allowing greater delicacy of touch from the

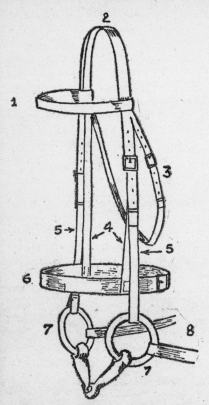

FIG. 11. THE
SNAFFLE

1. Browband.
2. Head Piece.
3. Throatlash.
4. Support of Cheek
   Piece of Noseband.
5. Cheek Strap of Bit
   Headstall.
6. Cavesson Noseband.
7. Snaffle Rings.
8. Snaffle Reins.

rider. The 'Fulmer' snaffle also has an unusually thick mouthpiece, which makes it less severe than a similar bit with a thin mouthpiece.

Basically, the snaffle bit acts upon the lips of the horse and 'bars' of his mouth – that is, the skin covering his lower jaw – and should be so adjusted that it touches the corners of his mouth without wrinkling them.

A description of the snaffle bridle would not be complete without mention of a useful adjunct to it, the dropped nose-band. This differs from the 'cavesson' noseband, which passes round the horse's nose above the bit, in that it is adjusted lower on the horse's head and is buckled below the bit, the back strap resting in the horse's chin groove. The front part of the dropped noseband should never be so low that it interferes with the horse's nostrils, nor should it be buckled uncomfortably tightly.

The dropped noseband is a useful piece of equipment in that it prevents the horse's opening his mouth wide in an attempt to evade the bit, and it helps the bit to act effectively in the horse's mouth. Like the snaffle bit with which – and with no other type of bit – it should be used, the dropped noseband is effective and therefore very popular for general and competitive riding.

The double bridle

Being more complicated than the snaffle bridle, in both action and use, the double bridle is not recommended for the novice rider. In fact, this type of bridle is tending to be used less nowadays for general riding and hunting, and is most often seen in the show ring and on horses trained for

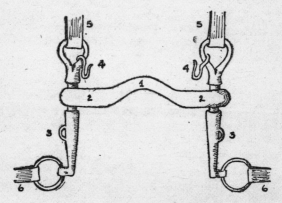

FIG. 12. THE DOUBLE BRIDLE

1. Port.	4. Curb-chain Hooks.
2. Cheeks.	5. Cheek Straps.
3. Lip-strap Eyes.	6. Bit or Curb Reins.

advanced dressage. The double bridle has two bits (hence its name), each with its own pair of reins; the bits are the bridoon and curb, and each has a separate headstall. The bridoon bit is similar to the snaffle in appearance and action, being a smooth, jointed, mouthpiece with a small ring at each end; it should bear on the corners of the horse's mouth without causing wrinkling and lies above the curb bit. To the rings are attached the bridoon or snaffle reins and the cheekpiece of its headstall.

The curb, sometimes referred to merely as "the bit", employs a quite different principle of action to that of the snaffle. The mouthpiece of the curb presses on the bars of the horse's mouth and the tongue (though the hump or "port" in the middle of the mouthpiece reduces this pressure considerably). The cheeks of a bit act on the lever principle, pressure on the curb rein tightening the curb chain round the horse's lower jaw, and also exerting a little pressure on the top of his head via the curb headstall. The relative intensities of these forces depend on the ratio of the length of the curb's cheek above and below the mouthpiece (the longer the more powerful, basically) and the tightness of the curb chain.

Even a short-cheeked curb is quite a strong bit and should be used with great delicacy of touch. The curb chain should always be twisted so that it lies flat in the horse's chin groove and a "chain" of flat leather or elastic material, or a rubber or sheepskin cover, may be used to make the action milder. When placed in the horse's mouth the curb comes slightly below the bridoon, so that it does not bear on the horse's lips.

The purpose of the bridoon in the double bridle is the normal control of the horse and to raise his head. The curb is used to bring his head in and induce him to flex his jaw. Thus it will be seen that it is possible to obtain better headcarriage and balance with a double bridle. With judicious use, better control of an unruly horse is sometimes possible, though some knowledge of the particular horse is desirable as certain animals are upset by the curb bit.

As mentioned before, the bit reins must be used delicately, with tact and understanding, as very great pain can be caused by their harsh use. Though many animals seem to perform well in a double bridle, it may not always be necessary to bring the curb bit into play on them – sometimes its mere presence will have the desired effect.

With regard to holding the reins of the double bridle for mounting, most people find it simpler to take up only the snaffle reins, leaving the curb reins alone until they are safely in the saddle, and this is a wise plan. The easiest way of holding all four reins in one hand is to have those of the bridoon on the outside, one rein passing outside the little finger, and the other inside the index finger; the curb reins will then pass between the little finger and the third, and between the third and second fingers.

An effective way of holding the reins in two hands for general work is for the bridoon reins to pass outside the little fingers and the bit reins between the little and the third fingers.

Pelham

In appearance the pelham is rather like the curb bit of the double bridle, with an additional ring on either cheek at the point where it is joined to the mouthpiece; this ring takes the bridoon or snaffle reins, occasionally called the 'cheek' reins.

The mouthpiece is generally smooth and may be gently curved ('mullen-mouthed' or 'half-moon') to allow more room for the horse's tongue. The pelham is theoretically a combination of the snaffle and curb bits and is best regarded as such when in use, the same care being exercised in the use of the curb reins. The pelham occupies a similar position in the horse's mouth to the curb bit.

The pelham bit may be used with two pairs of reins, or with one pair attached to leather loops joining the snaffle and curb rings. This principle is taken further with the popular 'Kimblewick', a bit with D-shaped rings, a straight mouthpiece with a low port, and curb chain. A pair of reins

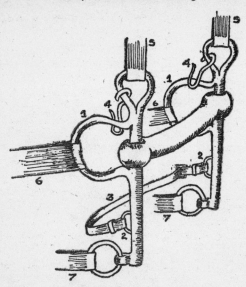

FIG. 13. THE PELHAM

1. Bridoon (Cheek) Rings.
2. Lip-strap Eyes.
3. Lip Strap.
4. Curb-chain Hooks.
5. Cheek Straps.
6. Bridoon, Snaffle or Cheek Reins.
7. Bit or Curb Reins.

is attached to the D-ring, so that the bit has a very mild curb action combined with that of a straight snaffle. Many horses go very kindly in the 'Kimblewick', just as many difficult animals respond very well to the pelham, and the former has the advantage of being relatively mild and easy for the rider, particularly the young rider, to manage.

Bridling

In bridling a horse the reins are first passed over his head on to his neck, then the right hand, holding the bridle at the top, is held above his head while the left hand places the bit in his mouth. Usually the horse will open his mouth if the bit is pressed lightly against it, but if he does not oblige, the thumb of the left hand, introduced into the corner of the

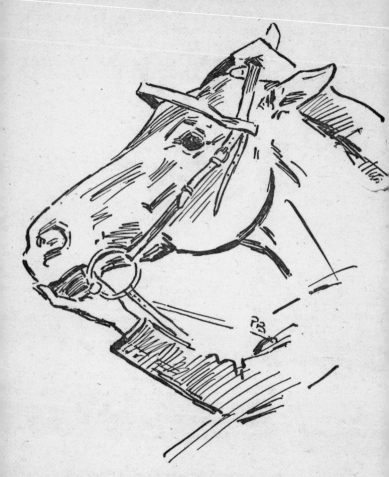

FIG. 14.   BRIDLING

The reins having been passed over on to the horse's neck, the
headpiece of the bridle is held by the right hand above his head.
The left hand places the bit in the mouth, while the right hand
lifts the bridle. The drawing shows the left thumb opening the
mouth, but with most horses the pressure of the bit against the
teeth is sufficient to do this.

mouth (behind his front teeth), invariably does the trick.
When the headstall has been placed over his head and his
ears made comfortable the throatlash and noseband are
fastened and, if there is one, the curb chain also. Already
looped on to the off-side hook, the curb chain is twisted so
that all the links lie flat before it is hitched on to the near-
side hook, and it should be sufficiently loose to allow two
fingers between it and the jaw. It should be noted that in the
double bridle the curb chain lies outside the snaffle – if it is
placed between the snaffle and the lips pinching is caused
and soreness results. In a pelham bridle the curb chain is
generally passed through the snaffle reins for the same
reason. When the curb is not brought into play the cheeks of
the bit should hang vertically. The lip-strap, a small, thin
strap, is passed through the loose link in the middle of the
curb chain and buckled to the cheek of the bit on either side,
fairly tightly.

Care and cleaning of bridles

All items of harness, whether metal or leather, require regular attention, not merely for the sake of appearance but to
prolong their life and strength; the folly of riding with
equipment that is worn or rotted, and is therefore likely to
give way unexpectedly, cannot be over-stressed. Keeping the
leather supple and the metalwork clean, if not polished, will
also add to the comfort of both horse and rider.

If the leather has become greasy, it should be well washed
with warm, not hot, water, before rubbing in saddle soap.
Never use detergent on leather, and use no more water than
is absolutely necessary, but some is unavoidable as a preliminary sponging is usually required to free the harness of
dirt.

Saddle soap will give leather a reasonable shine, but never
be tempted to make it really sparkle by using boot polish –
not only will it stain both you and the horse but it also tends
to make some harness leather dry out and crack. A regular
extra-special treatment with an oily or greasy leather dressing such as neatsfoot oil, 'Ko-Cho-Line' or 'Flexalan' is a

good idea though, especially to supple and darken down new leather or to protect harness before it is stored.

When cleaning harness do not forget that the underside is as important as the side you see. It is also wise to undo all the buckles regularly as it is at the buckles that most wear occurs. Besides checking for damage to the leather itself, remember to look for signs of the stitching's giving way, for this too can often be a weak point of harness.

The metal portions, particularly the bit, should be kept clean by washing and, since most are nickel or stainless steel, a rub with metal polish will make it bright. The links of the curb chain can be made to polish themselves very well if the chain is rubbed together in a duster.

It helps to get into the habit of cleaning the bridle as soon as it is taken off the horse. If time does not permit thorough cleaning immediately, make a point of at least washing the dirt from the bit and the grease from the leather. A damp cloth can be kept handy for the purpose and a few seconds spent on your return from a ride will save work later, when the grease and dirt have become hard and more difficult to remove.

16

Saddles and Saddling Up

The basic requirements of any saddle are the same: it must not allow any weight to be borne by the horse's spine, nor should it press on or pinch the animal's withers, and it must provide a comfortable and secure seat for the rider. The weight should be evenly distributed and carried by the muscles on either side of the backbone, leaving the animal's shoulders and loins quite free.

Thus we see the need for a saddle of the correct size and shape for any particular combination of horse and rider. Too broad a saddle will, with the rider's weight in it, bear upon the horse's spine and withers, while too narrow a one will pinch the withers. When mounted, the rider should be able to insert at least two fingers between the horse's withers and the underneath of the saddle arch, even when leaning forward.

Attention should also be paid to the stuffing of the panels of the saddle, which lie on the horse's back. If this stuffing is insufficient or has become spread and thin with use, there is a likelihood of the saddle's resting on the horse's backbone and withers and, since it is constructed on a metal, or occasionally wooden, frame or 'tree', it will readily produce sores, particularly if it rocks or moves when the horse is in action. Best of all such a worn saddle should be re-lined or re-stuffed but, alternatively, special pads, of felt, sheepskin, or fabric-covered foam rubber, called 'numnahs', are obtainable to keep the saddle off the spine; a folded blanket can also be used as a temporary measure. A numnah or blanket so employed should be lifted clear of the horse's spine when girthing up otherwise it will press down;

also, care should be taken that it is not wrinkled and is quite free of dirt or other material that can rub and cause soreness.

A common mistake in trying to solve the problem of a saddle that presses on the horse's withers is that of placing a pad under the front arch of the saddle; this is near useless, since the withers will still be bearing weight even though they are not in direct contact with the saddle arch.

Saddling up

The first steps in saddling up are to run the stirrup irons up and throw the girth, already buckled to the tabs on the right side of the saddle, back across the seat. This is largely for convenience and also to prevent the horse's being upset with unlucky blows from dangling girths or stirrups.

FIG. 15. SADDLING-UP

The final precaution against galling from wrinkling of the skin under the girth: stretching each foreleg in turn. It is also wise to run a finger down between the girth and the horse's side at each stage of tightening up. Note the position of the saddle: clear of the withers but not resting near the loins (which must always be free from pressure), girth in the 'girth place' and clear of the elbows.

Anyone who has watched a careless person carrying a saddle with the girth trailing miserably along in the mud, ending by stepping on the girth in negotiating the stable door and pitching headlong into the box (to the consternation of the occupant and mirth of the onlookers) might well take that unfortunate as an awful warning.

So, with the saddle neat and tidy, approach the horse on his near-side from the front, so that he can see what is coming to him, and place it gently on his back farther forward than it will be when finally girthed up. From this position the saddle can be slid back into its correct place and the lie of the hair will not be disturbed. When in position the saddle will be clear of the withers and the girth will lie in the girth place about four inches behind the elbows. Next the girth is passed underneath the horse and loosely buckled on to the appropriate girth tabs, the tightening-up being done gradually and finally completed just before mounting. Many animals develop a fine art of blowing themselves out in order that they may have a slack girth, so that it is frequently necessary to make several adjustments before the saddle is firm enough.

When tightening up, remember that a loose girth is as bad as an over-tight one, but it should only be tight enough to keep the saddle steady. Finally, run a finger down between the front of the girth and the horse's side to smooth any wrinkles of skin which could lead to discomfort and galling. And, as an additional precaution, lift each foreleg in turn and stretch it forward, to straighten out the horse's skin under the girth.

Cleaning saddles

In cleaning saddles special care should be given to those parts which come into direct contact with the horse, if soreness and galling are to be avoided. The tendency to pass lightly over them because they are safely out of sight must be resisted. The sweat and scurf should be sponged off a leather lining with warm water, then saddle soap or an oil dressing rubbed in, all surplus being removed with a clean

Fig. 16
THE SADDLE

Fig. A.
1. Pommel.
2. Seat.
3. Cantle.
4. Panel.
5. Spring Bar.
6. Flap.
7. Skirt covering Spring
   Bar.

Fig. B.
1. Sweat Flap.
2. Girth Leathers or
   Tabs.
3. Portion of Front
   Arch of Tree.

Fig. C.
Fitzwilliam
(Webbing)
Girth.

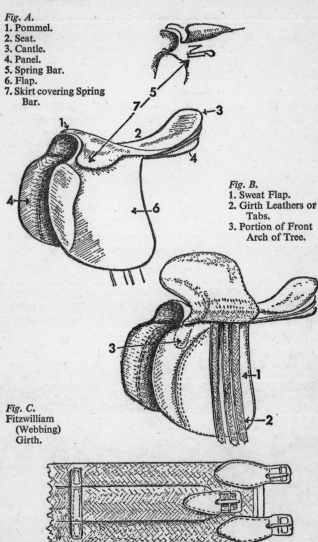

dry cloth. Linings of linen, serge or woollen fabrics require attention with a stiff brush to keep them clean and soft.

Girths made of webbing also require regular brushing, and those of leather should be treated in the same way as a leather saddle-lining. A very popular type of girth is the nylon-string one, which is readily washable and can be kept clean and soft without difficulty.

The girth is buckled to leather girth tabs and these and the sweat flaps and upper, leather-covered, surface of the lining should have saddle soap or harness oil well rubbed in. It is important to watch the holes in the girth tabs for wear, since constant use on the same holes will lead to their enlarging and, in time, possibly their breaking through at the edges.

The flaps of the saddle and the seat also require cleaning, the soap being thoroughly worked in and any surplus removed, otherwise it will soil the rider's clothes. Remember the undersides of the flaps, too.

When cleaning stirrup leathers, particular attention is necessary to the parts taking the irons and those passing over the bar on the saddle, as considerable wear may be found here. To alter these points of wear on stirrup leathers continually used at the same length they should be taken up a few inches at the buckle end every so often by the saddler.

Stirrup irons, like bits, are best made of stainless steel and, whether of nickel or stainless, should be treated in the same way, as described in the previous chapter.

17

Artificial Aids

In addition to those 'natural aids', legs, hands, and the rider's weight and voice, which were described in chapter 7, there are what are termed 'artificial aids', by which is meant such adjuncts as martingales, whips and spurs.

Standing martingale

The standing martingale is not necessary with a well-trained horse and need only be used on those animals which try to evade control by raising their heads high in the air. When used, the martingale should be adjusted so that the strap which passes from the horse's cavesson (never attach a standing martingale to a dropped noseband) noseband to the loop through which the girth passes has no effect until the animal raises its head unduly high. The use of a very tight standing martingale on horses that are expected to exert themselves over large fences is certainly not to be recommended, for in restricting the extent to which they can stretch head and neck the martingale discourages them from jumping with a proper 'bascule'.

Running martingale

The running martingale is similar in appearance to the standing, in that it has a neckstrap supporting a strap which loops on to the girth at one end. The other end of this strap, however, divides into two, each of which terminates in a small metal ring through which the rein passes.

An essential difference between the two types of martingale is that the standing type has an action entirely independent of the rider's hands while the running martingale

FIG. 17. THE STANDING MARTINGALE

The correct length for the Standing Martingale. It should be fitted so that it comes into operation only when the head is raised unusually high. The strap from the noseband passes through a neckstrap before looping on to the girth, in order to prevent its hanging dangerously low when the head is lowered.

has its effect on the reins. The latter ensures that the pull on the reins comes from the right direction, whatever the position of the rider's hands, and it may therefore help with a horse that is inclined to evade by raising its head. Because it runs along the rein, this type of martingale does not interfere with the freedom of movement of the horse's head and neck.

In saddling up, the neckstrap is placed over the horse's head and the girth is passed through the loop of the strap

which runs centrally between the horse's forelegs; the reins
are unbuckled at the end, passed through the rings, and
buckled up again. The running martingale should be adjusted so that it has not the slightest effect on the reins so
long as the rider's hands and the horse's head are placed
correctly. The neckstrap should not be too loose, and should
be of sound leather – it may provide a most useful emergency hand-hold for the rider.

Whip and spurs

A whip is a useful aid to help the rider's leg, and – used with
discretion – may occasionally give valuable service in the
correction of a disobedient horse. The whip, since its job is
to emphasize the leg aid, is always used behind the girth and
to use it the rider should put the reins in one hand, leaving
the whip hand free. Trying to use the whip with a hand
which is also holding a rein means that the horse feels the
whip down his side and at the same time receives a jerk in
the mouth. This just confuses the animal, the rider loses
balance and control, and if the horse is already being awk-
ward the situation goes from bad to worse.

The whip itself should be some 24 to 26 inches long, and
may be a simple cane, or some modification of this. It is
carried lying across the palm of the hand, so that a few
inches of its top end protrudes between the upper part of the
first finger and the thumb. The whip is held at its point of
balance, the top end pointing towards the horse's opposite
ear and its length lying along the rider's arm; this is important as the horse can see a surprising amount of his rider,
including a whip flapping about – which may make him
apparently unexplainably jumpy.

The hunting whip, is often misused for hacking and general
riding, for which it is neither the right length nor, without its
thong, correctly balanced. It consists of a rather heavy,
covered, stick with a right-angled hook of bone on one end
and a leather tab on the other. To the tab is attached a plaited
leather thong a couple of feet long with a silk or whipcord
lash on its end. The whip is carried with its tab upwards,

held at its point of balance just above the hook, and it should only be used for hunting, where the thong may be of use with hounds, and the crook helpful in dealing with gate catches. Without its thong the hunting whip is hopelessly unbalanced and difficult and uncomfortable to carry.

Spurs can be useful adjuncts, but should be used only by those who can use their legs independently, so will not give the horse an inadvertent dig in the ribs if they are thrown momentarily off balance. Even then, sharply rowelled spurs really have no place in modern riding, the short-necked, blunt variety being all that is required. Spurs should, of course, be used with great discretion. Both whips and spurs are banned usually from gymkhana races and similar events, and for general riding a short cane is all that is required.

18

Clothes for Riding

The most important factor as far as dress for riding is concerned is that it should be clean, neat and, as far as possible, correct. Newness and great expense do not necessarily make an outfit either 'right' or comfortable, and it is quite possible to look very smart in clothes acquired secondhand, or passed down from relatives and friends. Some things are indispensable, though, before you even begin to think about going riding.

Headgear

Beginning at the top, and with the most important item, it is difficult to over-emphasize the importance of wearing a hard hat for riding. The velvet-covered safety cap, with a re-inforced crown and complete with a chin-strap, is a must for children, and either this or a riding bowler (which is re-inforced and rather lower than its city brother) is advisable for grown-ups for general riding and hacking. If people realized how many serious head injuries, some with long-lasting – sometimes permanent – effects, were incurred during riding accidents, they would not consider riding or letting their children ride, without a hard hat which will at least reduce the extent of injury.

For safety caps there is a British Standard, which means that hats complying with the Standard carry the 'Kite' label. Should you be unfortunate enough to take a nasty fall on your head (or careless enough to let a horse walk on your hat) then don't forget that your hat should be discarded as the re-inforced crown will have done its job and may have been damaged in the process (without the hat that would have been your skull) so that a new hat is necessary. For this reason, and to keep your hat clean and smart, be sure to hang it up out of harm's way when you are not wearing it and don't just cast it down where a horse or pony may accidentally kick it.

Riding hats, either caps or bowlers, should be cleaned by brushing them with a clothes brush when they are dry. The fit of the hat should be close, and it is adjusted by means of the draw-string inside the crown. On your head the hat should be worn well down, never perched on the back of the head where it is ineffective as a protection and looks untidy. It is perhaps worth noting that for fast competitive riding, such as racing, point-to-pointing and the cross-country phase of combined training events, riders now have to wear proper safety helmets.

How your hair should be worn for riding is, of course, really up to you, but nothing looks more untidy than long tresses hanging loose. For a girl, tying your hair back out of the way is practical, because it prevents its getting into your eyes at some critical moment, and it is much more comfortable, too. The hair should be secured in a net, in pigtails, in a pony tail, or it may be put up, depending on its length and your own preferences; any of these methods will prevent its dangling round your collar. Your hair should not show under the peak of your riding cap, nor under the brim of a bowler either.

Footwear

Footwear for riding is also important from the safety angle. If you wear heel-less shoes they can allow your whole foot to pass through the stirrup iron with the result that your ankle may be trapped and you could be dragged, a very nasty occurrence. With such soft shoes it is also rather painful if the horse accidentally treads on your toe and though this is never a comfortable experience it is less unpleasant if you are wearing strong shoes or boots. These do not include shoes with prominent buckles or wellington boots, either of which may jam in the stirrup iron because of their width.

For riding, either walking shoes or jodhpur boots are the minimum acceptable, even if the rest of the outfit consists of jeans and a tatty shirt – and, of course, your hard hat. The short, usually elastic-sided, jodhpur boots are more comfortable and with jodhpurs they look smarter than shoes; whichever you wear, they should be cleaned regularly with boot polish. Brown is the preferred colour for jodhpur boots.

With breeches, full length boots of leather or rubber should be worn. The height of these long boots is important and the top should be well clear of the angle of the leg when the knee is bent, or else soreness will result. Either brown or black boots are worn. However, black 'butcher' boots of leather are considered the smartest and most comfortable, though they are expensive to buy and require considerable maintenance. Like all leather boots they should be kept on wooden trees – or, if you have no trees, packed with crumpled newspaper – to keep their shape. They are cleaned with water, dried with a cloth or leather and allowed to finish drying in a warm, but not hot, place before being polished with a suitable, good quality polish.

Garter straps are *de rigueur* with butcher boots, as with all long riding boots, to prevent their sagging and slipping. The garter is a narrow leather strap, the same colour as the boot, which is passed through a loop at the inside of the back of the boot and buckled around the leg. The buckle is worn to the front of the shin with the end of the strap cut short, and pointing to the outside.

Inside each boot will be found two webbing tabs, which are for the purpose of pulling the boot on, with the aid of boot hooks. When the boot is on, these tabs are tucked back in the leg, care being taken that they lie flat. To remove the boots a boot jack is of great assistance; failing this, someone else has to grab the heel of the boot and pull.

Rubber riding boots are a less expensive alternative to the more traditional leather ones, and they are smart and easily cleaned. However, they tend to be rather too hot in summer and cold in winter. Gaiters may be worn instead of long boots with breeches. Special ankle boots with extended tops, but never shoes, should be worn with them and the gaiters should be secured so that they cannot twist round the leg.

Jodhpurs and breeches

Jodhpurs and breeches of stretch nylon have the advantage that they are easy to wash and keep clean, and they are tough and wear well. Jodhpurs are acceptable for all ages of rider for casual hacking, though they are less popular with grown-ups than with children.

Adults prefer to wear breeches and full-length boots as these are smarter, particularly once you have stopped growing and they can be properly fitted. Both breeches and jodhpurs should be comfortable and well cut, fitting closely above and below the knee but without restricting movement in any way.

Jodhpurs are fitted from knee to ankle and, to make sure that they do not ride up, it is helpful to sew to the bottom of each leg an elastic strap which will pass under the instep of your boot. Breeches, finishing at about mid-calf level, are also more comfortable if continuations of a thinner material are added to them to prevent their pulling out of place. Breeches may fasten with buttons at the front of the knee, or with a modern contact adhesive fastening, but laces are not considered correct.

Drab is the best colour for breeches and jodhpurs. The insides of the knees of both are equipped with extra patches (strappings) of fabric or soft leather, to prevent excessive wear and to counteract any tendency to wrinkle.

Stretch nylon fabrics are washable and dry readily, so that there is really no excuse for wearing jodhpurs or breeches of this material in a dirty condition. Both from these and from non-washable fabrics (which have to be dry-cleaned when dirty) mud may be removed – once it is dry – with a stiff clothes brush. If you try to brush it while it is still wet you will only smear the mud into the cloth.

Jodhpurs and breeches should always be hung up on the cross bar of a coat hanger so that they do not crease; it is important to hang up these rather heavy garments as soon as you take them off, while they are still warm and while you think of it. Similarly, any small repairs, such as sewing on hooks or buttons, should be attended to before you put your clothes away, rather than at the last minute before you put them on.

If you do a lot of riding, and perhaps look after your own horse or pony, the wear and tear of daily use may prove too much for such costly items as breeches and jodhpurs. Slacks or jeans are more economical and often easier to wash so that many people wear them for day to day riding. They do not, of course, look as smart as the 'proper thing'. They tend to wrinkle uncomfortably on the inside of the knee, and the lower leg may work up. Even so, they are practical and cheap, though they should always be clean and tidy.

Coats

The riding jacket is specially cut so that it is full in the skirt and lies neatly over the saddle when you are mounted. Rather longer than a sports jacket, and with either one or two vents at the back, it has pockets set on a slant. For most occasions a tweed or quiet check coat is most suitable and this may be worn with jodhpurs, or with breeches and black or brown boots.

A black jacket, or occasionally dark grey or navy blue, may be worn with breeches and butcher boots and is most suitable for smart occasions. Black coats should not really be worn for casual riding or hacking, nor with jodhpurs, and are not therefore strictly correct wear for children. Since they are harder to keep looking smart than tweed jackets, there seems little point in young people wearing them.

All jackets should, of course, be clean, and require regular brushing to keep them so, with dry-cleaning occasionally. They should be put on a hanger when not being worn to keep them in shape, and the pockets emptied to prevent their sagging. When riding, try to avoid carrying large, lumpy objects such as apples or bottles in the pockets of your coat as these are dangerous should you have a fall, will make your jacket more susceptible to being torn by brambles and the like, and look very untidy. It also looks very untidy to wear your jacket undone; if you are too hot it is best to take the coat off.

For ordinary riding and exercising a wind-cheater is a more economical alternative to a proper riding jacket, and is quite acceptable. Because these garments tend to flap dangerously, and could thus frighten or surprise your mount, it is best to wear them done up, particularly in windy weather.

Shirts and pullovers

For casual riding, a high-necked pullover in a practical, dark colour, is very suitable and it may be worn under a tweed coat in very cold weather.

For smart occasions for young people a white or cream shirt should be worn under the coat, with a collar and tie, the tie secured with a tie-pin so that it cannot flap about. If the points of your shirt collar are long they too should be pinned down. In cold weather a woollen waistcoat or a suitable pullover is a useful addition to the outfit.

For adults either a shirt, collar and tie or a coloured or patterned stock is worn with a tweed jacket. A stock should, of course, be correctly and neatly tied, and secured with a pin. With a black coat a grown-up should wear a 'hunting tie', which is basically a stock of white piqué (stiff ribbed cotton). Tying a hunting tie correctly requires some practice, and it is considered incomplete without a pin to secure it.

Gloves and spurs

Gloves should be worn on smart occasions, and to keep your hands warm and dry. Plain leather gloves look neat and allow plenty of feeling through them, though they are sometimes inclined to slip. String gloves are the favourites for riding in wet weather and they do not slip on the reins as do gloves of other materials. They are made of coarse knitted cotton and should be a little bigger than would normally be worn to allow for movement of the rider's fingers. Leather gloves are sometimes usefully modified with string material substituted on the insides of the fingers, overcoming their tendency to slip on wet reins. If you intend being out for long in very wet weather it may be helpful to carry a spare pair of string or woollen gloves tucked flat under the girth straps where the saddle flap will keep them dry.

Spurs, of the short, blunt 'dummy' type are the correct wear with butcher boots for smart occasions although for the novice rider and for hacking and some competitive riding it may be preferable, even if not strictly correct, to wear the boots without spurs. It is not desirable to wear spurs with jodhpur boots, though this is occasionally done.

The spurs themselves are worn with the blunt ends pointing downwards, and high up on the boot at the level of the seam where foot and leg meet; the longest arm of the spur is worn on the outward side and the buckle of the spur's strap should be to the outside. The free end of the spur strap should be cut short, and the spurs, like the boots they adorn, should be clean and polished.

Outfits for some occasions

When smartness is not required, as for example when you are out hacking or exercising your pony as part of the daily routine the following applies. You must wear a hard hat and walking shoes or jodhpur boots (clean); otherwise, jeans and a pullover and wind cheater are acceptable; your hair should be tied out of the way. You should be neat and clean.

When proper dress is required of young people, as for example for a riding lesson, a local pony show or competition or a Pony Club rally: you need your hard hat, shirt with a collar and suitable tie (Pony Club tie if you are a member), the tie secured with a pin or badge, and a tweed jacket; jodhpurs and jodhpur boots or walking shoes; string gloves and a cane; again, your hair should be tied back if long.

For adults 'ratcatcher' or 'undress' is suitable for a riding lesson, smart hacking and some competitive work. It may also be worn for hunting with some modifications (namely a bowler rather than a cap and a hunting whip, with thong and lash, rather than a cane): a riding cap or bowler, a tweed hacking jacket, a shirt with collar and tie or a coloured stock with a pin; drab breeches and boots of black or brown with spurs (strictly correct, but not required in most instances) and proper garter straps; gloves and a cane.

Riding in wet weather

For those who intend to do much riding in Britain a riding macintosh is probably a good investment. It is specially cut with a full skirt to give protection to your legs and to the saddle and is usually fitted with leg straps to prevent its flapping about or rucking up. These garments are generally made of a heavy and very durable waterproof fabric and though they are rather expensive to buy they last for many years and are a good investment. The same may be said of a riding apron, also made of macintosh, and cut so that it is secured at the waist, under the coat, and attached to the rider's knees to prevent their being soaked.

Raincoats of gaberdine and similar fabrics which are not made for riding do not give the same protection that a proper riding macintosh does, though they are a good deal better than nothing. Care should be taken about using waterproofs of plastic and similar materials for riding as these may flap and blow about and the noise could frighten the horse. They also look untidy.

If the weather is showery it may be convenient to roll up your mac, outer side outwards, into a long sausage and secure it across the front of the saddle, tying it with cord to the D-rings on either side of the pommel. Alternatively, carry the macintosh as a parcel on your back.

These notes on clothes are intended only to set the novice rider on the right path, the standards of dress for riding not being nearly as rigid as they once were. At the same time, the horseman or horsewoman should observe customs in riding dress as far as possible, for many of these 'rules' have practical reasons behind them. Remember always that in clothes, as in everything else connected with the horse, neatness and unobtrusiveness are the keywords.

To take sensible safety precautions like wearing proper protective headgear and boots for riding, is only common sense, as such measures can greatly reduce the risk – and consequent difficulties for yourself and other people – of injuring yourself seriously should you have the misfortune of a nasty tumble.

19

Hacking and Riding on the Road

In this book we have had in mind the instruction necessary for those who wish to go hacking, and enjoy doing so. 'Hacking' is the term used to describe ordinary, everyday riding for pleasure and exercise, and this will cover riding both on roads and bridlepaths; you may also ride in an enclosed 'school', where you will no doubt undertake your early lessons, and where you may go later as you try to improve your riding and learn more about what makes your horse 'tick'.

In this imperfect world it is seldom impossible to avoid roads completely, and in many parts of the country much of your hacking may have to be along the public highway. This is not very satisfactory, either for you and your horse or for the passing motorists. From the rider's point of view, having always to be concentrating on the passing traffic is not ideal, though essential, and from the motorist's angle you should remember that you and your horse do present an obstruction which has to be carefully avoided. For this reason you should always try to ride your horse as close to the roadside as possible – on the verge if you can – and never ride in more than a single file where you could interfere with other road-users and, of course, endanger yourselves by so doing.

Most motorists are considerate to horses and slow down and give them a wide berth. Some, however, are not, and you must always be prepared for the driver who whistles past you, 'knocking the mud off your boots with his wing mirror'. This sort of driver will always make the horse jump, and – if you are not ready to soothe and steady him – he may set off at a smart pace in the wrong direction. Such thoughtlessness on the part of drivers is rare, though, and the courtesy of the majority should be acknowledged by thanking them with a wave or a smile. If you do not do this can you really be surprised if they decide not to bother to slow down for horses they pass in future?

On the public highway the rider should keep to the left, and should follow the road signs which apply to motorists. (For a good example of how this should be done, observe the officers of the Mounted Police riding their horses through dense city traffic, waiting at traffic lights and pedestrian crossings, as must any other vehicle.) The horseman must also signal his intentions to other road-users, that is, to motorists and pedestrians, and the signals he should use in the U.K. are those laid down in the 'Highway Code'. To indicate that he intends to turn right, the rider extends his right arm horizontally well before he intends to make the manoeuvre, and he should always remember to look behind him carefully before turning across a road. Under these circumstances make sure that you have the horse well under your control, and that you are prepared to stop him and stand and wait until the road is clear; it is also worth noting that horse's iron shoes make a surprising noise on the hard road, to which you become accustomed as you ride, so never rely on just listening for a vehicle behind you – a cyclist or a powerful car can easily creep up without your noticing it.

To turn left, you signal by holding your left arm horizontally. You will seldom need to signal your intention to slow down and stop, but the signal for this is given with your right hand, moving up and down.

You may, however, find that it is sometimes necessary to beckon motorists on as, for example, when your horse has been playing up and has settled enough to allow the cars to pass. Round blind bends it may help the motorist if you beckon him on if the road is clear, but be very careful about this; be quite sure that the road really is clear, for a nasty accident could result if it is not.

When making hand signals, remember that all the movements of your arms are clearly visible to the horse, and may upset a nervous animal. In such a case less obtrusive hand signals may be better, but they must, of course, still be clear to other road-users.

Traffic-shy horses

With modern roads as they are, it is a fool's game to ride a traffic-shy horse on the road. Some horses are young and nervous of motor traffic (especially lorries, which tend to make a considerable noise), mainly because they are unaccustomed to it. For these animals, grazing in a field close to a main road provides a good preliminary to early trips on the road; for these excursions a steady equine companion which can be ridden between the youngster and the road will considerably reduce the risk of serious trouble. And, as in all animal training, make haste slowly, and if you are in any doubt about the youngster's reaction to traffic, delay taking him out on his own for a while longer.

If you find yourself on a horse that is traffic-shy there are some important points to remember. A disconcerting, and very dangerous, trick that some such horses have is to take a look at an oncoming dustcart or the like and without any warning to wheel round and run for it. If the rider is not prepared for this reaction he finds himself careering along at a fast gallop and on the wrong side of the road. So, you need to bear in mind the possibility that the horse may spin round, and be prepared when you first see a potential hazard to drive him on strongly with your legs, with the reins short and a strong feel on his mouth. If he does wheel round, then do your best to bring him round again full circle, and drive him forward strongly and, if there is no gateway where you can take him off the road while the lorry goes by, you may have to dismount and lead him past it. And, if the driver has stopped for you, don't forget to thank him for his kindness.

Riding at night

Riding in the dark is also a pastime to be avoided if you possibly can. For, though you can see perfectly well, remember that you and your horse, are almost completely invisible to the motorist until he is really too close to you to take avoiding action; this is particularly so when he is watching the lights of other cars.

A red reflector or lamp on your right hand stirrup may help a little, but really does not give sufficient warning, nor does a white handkerchief tied to the horse's tail – though of course either is better than nothing.

An added danger when you are riding at night is that the headlights of vehicles approaching from behind cast curious, moving, shadows in the left hand hedge and verge, and these may make even a staid animal shy unexpectedly, and out into the road, with possibly disastrous result. Unfortunately, the fact has to be faced nowadays that you really cannot go further in a day than you can ride in daylight hours. And, if it looks as if you will not be back before dark, the sensible thing to do is try to stable the animal overnight, or else accept the inevitable and go by horsebox.

In case of accident . . .

If you are unfortunate enough to be involved in an accident with horses on the road, or anywhere else for that matter, the most important thing to remember is not to panic – this will just make things worse. Try to size up the situation quickly, and do what you can to prevent it deteriorating further. One particular danger in an accident involving a horse is that the animal will become quite terrified and get loose, so make sure that that cannot happen. After that has been done, see about calling what medical and veterinary help you need, and while you are waiting for that to arrive make any injured people (they come first) and animals as comfortable as you can.

In any accident on the road where people are injured the police should be called, and this is also a good idea where any claims are likely to be made for damages. Do not forget that, in a road accident, you may know all too well that it has occurred but other people coming along the road will not, so try to put up some sort of warning if there is any obstruction of the highway.

Getting off the road

Such dire warnings about the hazards of the road may seem to be taking the matter of horses and motor traffic too seriously, but the hazards of the road are such that the greatest of care must be taken. Where, then, can the rider relax and enjoy his riding? There are many bridlepaths all over the country which offer you an opportunity to give your full attention to the horse, and really to see the countryside. Most bridlepaths are kept clear and are well-marked by the local council; they, like the roadside verges, also offer a chance to get on to soft going and ease the horse's legs a little.

Horses' legs do not benefit from the ' 'ammer, 'ammer, 'ammer on the 'ard 'igh road' and, if you must trot on the road it is worth remembering that it should be a steady, controlled pace, both to minimize jarring and to reduce the risk of slipping. On the non-metalled tracks of the bridlepaths you can safely let your horse go on rather faster if you so wish. There is a great temptation, though, when you leave the 'ard 'igh road for the bridleway – where you do have right of way – to forsake the path for the neighbouring farmland – where you do not. If you want to ride on such land it is only civil to ask permission of its owner first, and to remember that much hard work goes into growing crops, and trampling over them on your horse is a far from considerate act.

Another point concerning consideration for others in the country. Though horses may not be ridden on footpaths, the pedestrian has as much right as the horseman to enjoy the peace and quiet of the bridleway and it is most unpleasant, when strolling along on a sunny afternoon, to be met by a cavalry charge of horsemen which spray one from

head to foot with liquid mud; nothing could be better cal-
culated to set other users of the countryside against riders.

Fields and bridlepaths quite often bring gates into the pic-
ture. Gates, generally speaking, are not ornaments but lead
sober and useful lives which implies that they have a job to
do. Cattle, and all animals for that matter, seem able to scent
an open gate from afar and make their way unerringly to it
and the forbidden land which lies beyond it. So remember

FIG. 18. OPENING GATES

When the gate opens outwards, the horse is placed close to it with
his tail towards the hinges; the fastening is unlatched and the gate
is pushed open and held until the horse is safely through. When the
gate opens inwards the horse is placed in a similar position, but
with his quarters farther away to allow the gate to be pulled open
and for him to pass round. The rider himself will, of course, have
to be closer to the fastening of this gate.

this and co-operate with gates in their mission in life, and leave them as you find them. It is no difficult feat to open and close gates from the back of a horse (nor is it really such a great hardship to dismount to attend to a gate that is being unco-operative, but such are in the minority).

To open a gate that swings outwards, ride up closely (with the horse's tail towards the hinges and his head to the fastening) unlatch it and push it open, taking care that it does not swing back before the horse is through. Closing this gate presents no difficulty, as the rider simply puts his horse alongside and pushes it shut, making sure that the catch engages.

When opening a gate that swings inwards towards the rider the horse is ridden up close, his body at a convenient angle to it to allow it to be unfastened, pulled open and held back until the horse has passed through. When through the gate the horse is turned so that he is parallel with the opening, facing away from the hinged end and the rider opposite the fastening. In this position the rider can lean over and draw the gate shut with the aid of his whip without much manoeuvring.

It will be found that many horses are very anxious to assist in opening and closing gates when this can be done by pushing against them with the chest or by a vigorous thrust from the nose. Some, again, become very proficient at undoing all types of fastenings and this would be a very useful accomplishment if it were not also practised in the stable.

Leading horses

When leading a horse on the road you should keep to the left with yourself between the traffic and the animal. (This became the practice in 1976. Prior to that date, you were recommended to face the oncoming traffic.) To lead the horse the reins should be taken over his head, and held in both hands, as shown in the illustration. If the horse is not wearing a bridle, he should be controlled by means of a stout, properly adjusted, headcollar with a rope of suitable length (not a piece of string) so that you will be able to cope

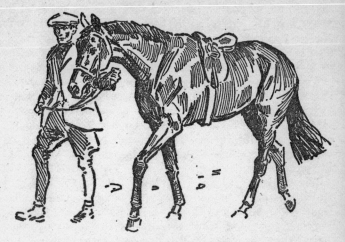

Fig. 19. COMING HOME

The drawing illustrates many points which deserve attention: after a long or tiring ride, dismount, run up the stirrup irons, slacken the girths and lead for the last mile; this eases the horse and allows him to cool off gradually. It is also often a welcome opportunity for the rider to stretch his legs. For safety, lead the horse on the left-hand side of the road, close to the edge, and keep yourself between him and the traffic. Walk level with and close to his head, the reins in the left hand, fairly close to the bit, allowing normal movement of the head, their free end taken in the right hand.

in case of difficulty. With a horse that is carrying a saddle, the stirrups should be run up the leathers so that they are out of the way, and the girths may be slackened to ease the animal.

When riding one horse and leading another, you should keep to the left of the road, with the ridden horse between the led one and the traffic. The rider holds the reins of the led horse in his bridle-hand, along with those of the horse he is riding. Some people prefer to use the right hand on the reins of their own horse and when a frisky horse is being led this is probably the safer way, the reins being held short and if the led animal becomes troublesome and tries to break away they can be slackened out at first, the horse being brought back to hand gradually. It is necessary to give to him in this way at first to prevent the reins' being jerked completely out of the hand by a sudden movement, or even the rider's being pulled from the saddle. With two hands busy with the reins, however, there is nothing left for signals to other motorists – except the expression on the rider's face, which may convey all too much!

One mistake that should not be made when leading a horse, from the ground or from another animal, is that of casually looping the reins over one finger; even though the horse may be absolutely quiet, he may still take fright suddenly and then – snap! – goes a finger. But then it is not the finger you should worry about, painful as it is, but that you may lose the horse as well. And, moreover, though you are worried enough already about what may happen to the horse while he is loose, particularly on a busy road, do not forget that you are also liable, legally, for his actions. This means that if he should gallop into a main road and cause a serious accident you could find yourself in a position where you have to pay compensation to those injured, or whose vehicles are damaged, in the incident. It is easy to get insurance which will cover third party damage – such cover often comes along with normal household insurance policies – and the insurance is not expensive. It is very foolish not to purchase this third party cover if you own or ride horses.

20

Pony Trekking and Trail Riding

Many people who have never ridden a horse before in their lives make their first attempts at riding in the course of a pony trekking holiday and – what is more – enjoy it very much. One of the charms of pony trekking is that it is un-hurried, allowing riders to proceed at their leisure through the very beautiful scenery in which most centres are situated. Because of the slow speed, the horses being ridden mostly at the walk with occasional periods of jogging or cantering, the novice rider is not at a disadvantage.

For those who have little experience of caring for horses the holiday which consists of a series of daily treks from a centre is probably the most suitable. Staying at a hotel, hostel or farmhouse, the riders go out each morning, taking with them a packed lunch, and return in the late afternoon. This involves a number of hours in the saddle and can be quite tiring, so that it is not recommended in most instances for people under about fourteen years of age, who generally prefer other types of riding holiday.

The amount of instruction given to riders and the length of each day's ride is usually adjusted according to the ex-pertise of the trekkers, though about twenty miles would be covered in a full day's trek. The horses used for this type of work are usually of the cobby type, such as Highland ponies, Fell ponies and Welsh Cobs, which have no difficulty in negotiating rough and rocky terrain. They are usually quiet, too, and unworried by inexpert handling; knowing the rides so well it is said that some could go round the normal trek routes without human guidance at all!

Many trekking centres are very well run, and most provide a brochure with details of the facilities offered, the ponies, the scenery and, of course, the cost. Regrettably, not all centres provide the excellent facilities they imply in their advertising pamphlets and some do not reach even a moderate standard, their ponies being in poor condition, saddlery worn out and ill-fitting, and supervision and instruction either inadequate or completely lacking. To help in choosing a trekking centre the British Horse Society and the Ponies of Britain Club both run Approval Schemes, which cover inspection of ponies and saddlery and assessment of the standard of supervision offered. Inquiries, with a stamped, self-addressed envelope, should be sent to 'The Ponies of Britain', Brookside Farm, Ascot, Berkshire.

Pony trekking is always fun, and is a good way to spend a holiday. Many centres offer a package deal and, if you are worried about the cost, it may be more economical to go in, or to arrange, a party with a block booking, particularly if you choose a time outside the most popular summer season. But in comparing costs do not be taken in by prices well below the average, for they may mean that something is skimped as it is never cheap to keep ponies and harness in good and serviceable condition, nor to employ competent staff.

Clothes for trekking

The expensive and specialized clothes worn for most types of riding are not required for trekking, and they could be a disadvantage. The clothes should, of course, be neat and tidy and not flap about in a way which might frighten the horse, but they should be comfortable for walking as well as riding. Jeans are very suitable wear (they do not ruck up at slow speeds) as are riding trousers or jodhpurs of light material; beware of heavy fabrics which will not dry overnight if you get caught in a downpour. Shorts are not suitable for pony trekking, though, as soreness may result from pinching of the bare skin. On the feet, laced walking shoes or short boots, such as jodhpur boots, are the most comfortable and with breeches long socks and walking shoes are preferable to full-length riding boots which seldom allow one to walk very far in comfort. Plimsolls or gum boots are not safe for any sort of riding.

A cotton shirt or a high-necked pullover, depending on the weather, is the most comfortable wear on top, with an anorak or wind-cheater in case of rain. The latter leaves the knees unprotected and to prevent their being soaked a pair of plastic or PVC over-trousers may prove useful. Alternatively, a riding mac which covers the knees and saddle is comfortable, though rather heavy to carry during sunny intervals.

For young people a hard hat is a must, and in really wet weather a sou-wester can be pulled over the hat to keep it and the head it covers dry. String gloves are also useful to keep hands warm and prevent the reins slipping, and when they are not in use they can be carried conveniently tucked under the girth straps. Other small extras which may prove useful include a penknife with a blunt marline spike, which can be used as a hoof pick in emergency, a length of string and a small haversack in which to carry your lunch. If you are proposing to travel without a guide, then navigating equipment, maps and a compass, are also necessary.

More experienced riders, some of whom could find trekking too leisurely, may find tours on horseback more challenging. The tour is generally made from a base and, in the case of 'post-trekking', each night is spent at a different, pre-arranged lodging where the ponies can be stabled or turned out in a field. This version of trekking is not suitable for the complete novice as quite considerable practical experience of pony-care is needed if the animals are to be kept fit throughout the journey.

The same applies, but even more so, to mounted expeditions, where riders carry their own lightweight camping gear and are completely self-sufficient for the duration of the tour. Participants in such expeditions may be eligible for an Award under the Duke of Edinburgh's Scheme.

There are many parts of Great Britain which are suitable for pony trekking, including many of the wilder areas of

Scotland and Wales, Yorkshire, the Fells and, in the south, Exmoor, Dartmoor and the New Forest. Ireland also has much attractive country for trekking and there are some places further afield, such as Spain and Norway. In most parts of Britain and Ireland 'riding holidays' are also offered, and these are especially recommended for children who might find whole days' trekking rather tiring. On these holidays instruction in riding and stable management is mixed with hacking and gymkhana games during the day, and there may also be organized, pony-oriented, activities in the evening. Details of centres offering this sort of holiday are also available from the Ponies of Britain organization.

Endurance riding

In Britain a riding sport which is increasing in popularity with some horse owners is long distance riding. This is a test of the fitness of the horse and his rider and involves covering a set distance, usually over pleasant but fairly difficult tracks or trails, at a specified pace. As well as being a test of the horse's stamina and the rider's horsemanship the events are very enjoyable and seem to encourage comradeship among the participants. In most events awards are made on class basis, rather than in set placings.

Major events in Britain would require riders to cover some fifty miles on the first day and twenty-five on the second, both at an average speed of about eight miles an hour. Stringent veterinary checks before, during and after a ride ensure that no animal is over-taxed and the physical condition of the horses which finish decides their classification. An advantage of this sport for many people, is that any horse which is physically sound is suitable as success depends more on the rider's hard work in getting his horse fit than on the animal's inherent ability.

British 'endurance riding' is derived from the American sport of competitive trail riding. Some of these events are races against the clock over long distances, fifty or a hundred miles, of sometimes very difficult terrain. Veterinary checks play an important part in these events, too, in deciding the winner and placings. Other American trail rides may require competitors to cover a relatively short distance, perhaps a hundred miles in three days, and placings depend much more on the condition of the animals at the end.

'Western' riding

In trail riding, or riding across unfenced country the 'Western', or cowboy, style of riding finds its métier. It is distinct from the English riding described in this book and though the American style is seldom seen in Britain it is gaining a little in popularity, particularly for endurance riding events.

Western riders tend to encourage their horses to move in a relaxed fashion, which will allow them to cover long distances with minimum effort. In addition to transport, American ranch horses' duties did, and still do to some extent, include the driving, 'cutting out' (or separating one from the bunch) and roping of cattle and the training, riding and harnessing of the horses is all done with these purposes in mind.

The Western saddle is noticeably different from the English one, being much heavier and equipped at the front with a horn to which the lasso is attached for 'rope-work'. The saddle also has a high cantle, so that the rider is held more firmly and he rides with rather longer stirrups and his knees straight. The horse is trained to respond to the feel of the rein on his neck, and to the rider's leg and weight-shifting aids rather than to the direct reining that is used in English riding. In consequence the rider lets the reins hang slightly loose and the horse carries his head more naturally.

The bits used in Western riding are basically of the curb type, with long cheeks, sometimes eight or nine inches, and a leather curb strap rather than a chain; no snaffle rein is used. A different type of bridle which arouses some interest is the Hackamore (the name is derived from the Spanish *la jaquima*, meaning noseband) which has no bit. Instead it has a curb device which tightens the noseband or, alternatively, a 'bosal', a braided leather noseband which allows pressure to be exerted directly on the horse's nose and the side of his face.

Training a horse Western style is not as easy as many people seem to think, and takes as much time and skill as training a horse to work English style. Even if you use a hackamore a horse can still suffer if he is ridden heavy handedly, becoming 'hard-nosed', and though a well-trained horse is under perfect control in such a bridle it is perhaps unwise to venture onto busy British roads with no other means of control than a bosal on a horse or pony which has not been thoroughly schooled to this form of restraint.

21

Shoeing and Care of the Horse's Feet

Though the horse's feet may seem far from the areas concerning the rider there is too much truth in the old saying 'No foot, no horse' for the subject of shoeing to be neglected.

The shoe is necessary to protect the horse's hoof from excessive wear and soreness resulting from work on hard surfaces, for within the horny case of the hoof lie delicate and very sensitive living tissues surrounding the bones of the foot. In view of this it may at first seem strange that such an apparently brutal procedure as nailing an iron shoe to the hoof should be acceptable. The process of fitting and nailing on the shoe is, however, a highly skilled one and, despite a number of trials with other materials, such as plastic and rubber, iron remains the most satisfactory for horse shoes.

To understand the attention needed by the foot it is necessary to know a little of its construction and the functions of the various parts. The horny hoof is equivalent to the human finger-or toenail and, like them, is always growing so that when the shoe protects it from the natural wear which would keep it to its proper length it has to be pared down by the farrier at regular intervals. Usually this trimming is done every three or four weeks, whether or not new shoes are needed, the shoes being removed, the feet pared and the old shoes replaced, or new ones put on. If this regular attention by the farrier is neglected the foot becomes misshapen and cannot bear the animal's weight satisfactorily.

The shoe is nailed to the bearing surface of the 'wall', the thick outer layer of horn which is constantly growing downwards. It joins, at the ground surface, the 'sole' of a rather thinner horn which flakes away naturally and, unlike the wall, does not need paring. Where sole and wall meet there is the 'white line', used by the farrier as an indication of the thickness of the wall to which he is nailing the shoe.

The triangular 'frog' is an elastic structure which acts as a cushion to reduce concussion and as an anti-slip device. It should be well-developed and able to perform its natural functions if the horse is being properly shod.

The basis of good shoeing is that the shoe is always made to fit the foot, the foot never being pared so that it fits the shoe. This is the great advantage of 'hot' shoeing, the new shoe being heated till it is red hot, tested for fit on the horse's hoof and then modified while still malleable. Unexpectedly, most horses are quite unconcerned when the hot iron is placed on their feet and clouds of acrid smoke billow round them. The shoe is not actually nailed to the horse's foot until it has been cooled.

'Cold' shoeing, where the shoe is not heated or materially altered to fit the horse's foot, is obviously a less desirable method. Whichever way a horse is shod, the bearing surface of the wall must be level so that the shoe rests on it all the way round without 'showing daylight'. The minimum number of nails needed to keep the shoe on should be used, and they are driven through the wall at an angle, the farrier using the sound and feel of the hammer striking the nail to guide him. The ends of the nails come out of the wall on its outside surface a few inches above the ground and their points are twisted off, the 'clenches' or ends being hammered smooth and flat.

In the stable a regular routine should be observed for the care of the horses' feet and it is in carrying out this routine that small troubles may be discovered and more serious damage thus prevented.

'Picking out' the horse's feet is an important part of grooming. By 'picking out' is meant removing all dirt and

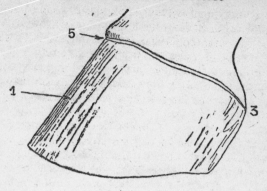

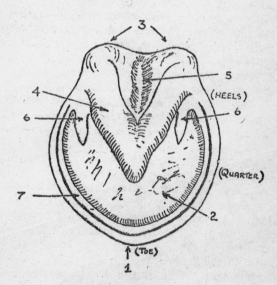

FIG. 20.   THE HOOF

Key, applicable to both drawings –

1. Wall.
2. Sole.
3. Bulbs of Heels.
4. Frog.

5. Coronet Band.
6. Bars of Foot.
7. 'White Line'.

stones with a blunt-pointed hook called a hoof-pick. The hoof-pick is drawn from the heel to the toe and should not be used with more force than is necessary to clear the hoof, particularly at the sides and in the central cleft of the frog. On returning to the stables after a ride the feet should be picked out again to remove any stones that may have become lodged, and it is wise always to carry a hoof-pick for this purpose when riding.

While picking out the horse's feet the condition of the shoes and state of growth, or over-growth, of the feet can be noted so that the farrier can be booked in good time. As temporary measures, risen clenches should be hammered flat again to prevent injury to the opposite leg, though once a shoe has become very loose or has spread it is best not to ride the horse until he has been re-shod. Never be tempted to try to 'put in a nail' to secure a loose shoe, or to do your own farriery – the chances are a hundred to one that you will lame your horse, possibly permanently.

22

Horses for the Handicapped

Learning to ride is not a skill that is particularly easy for anyone to acquire. So perhaps it comes as a surprise to learn that riding is proving to be a most enjoyable and valuable sport for disabled people who can move, in many cases, only with the aid of crutches or a wheelchair.

The idea of riding for the disabled was suggested by the success of Lis Hartel, a Danish rider who won the Silver Medal for dressage at the Helsinki Olympics even though she was otherwise chairbound as a result of polio. In Norway, experiments with riding for the disabled proved that it was beneficial, and in the late 'fifties some groups were formed in Britain. Now there is a large, and growing, number of groups of voluntary helpers providing riding for handicapped people; they belong to the Riding for the Disabled Association, a National organization whose patron is HRH Princess Anne, herself a most successful Three-Day-Event rider.

Benefits of the special riding sessions are many, the riders – mentally or physically handicapped – acquiring a new and delightful sense of freedom and achievement in the control of such a large animal. Contact with the living animal seems to improve confidence, as does the chance to look down on other people, for a change. Enjoyment is a big benefit, too, and disabled riders look forward very much to their lessons; being able to ride a pony, which many normal children would like to do but can't, helps a little towards compensating for a severe handicap, particularly in a young person.

Some riders need special equipment, one example is provision of foot-reins – with which he manages very well – for a boy who has no arms, and short-wave radio for communication with the blind. Apart from the boost to morale, the riders benefit from the continual movement of all muscles which riding demands and it is thus a very valuable form of physiotherapy, and it is accepted as such by the Chartered Society of Physiotherapists. The value of riding therapy is also accepted medically.

Groups are nearly always short of helpers and new volunteers, who are willing to give up a few hours a week, are always welcome. Though previous experience with horses is not necessary (though it is an advantage) helpers need to be adults or mature teenagers and they must, of course, be enthusiastic. They work up to three helpers per rider, either leading the horse or walking one on each side, to give assistance as it is needed. Work is done mainly at slow paces and the horses and ponies are chosen for their quietness; it is said that the animals even seem to sense that special care is needed with their disabled passengers.

Sessions are held at private houses, in one or two specially built centres or at riding schools, many of whose proprietors are very generous over the loan of facilities. A period of riding instruction and exercises in the saddle is followed by gymkhana games, such as a mounted version of 'grandmother's footsteps', and often a country ramble. A happy, relaxed atmosphere is the rule, for riders and helpers.

Affiliated to the British Horse Society, the Riding for the Disabled Association is a registered Charity with its Secretary's Office at the National Equestrian Centre, Kennilworth, Warwickshire CV8 2LR. An interesting concept, successfully developed into a growing movement, riding for the disabled is surely worthy of support by all those who can enjoy not only their riding but their daily lives free from handicaps. It provides an opportunity for disabled people to enjoy being with horses and to participate in one of the few sports which can give them as much pleasure as it gives those more fortunate.

Index

OUR PUBLISHING POLICY

HOW WE CHOOSE

Our policy is to consider every deserving manuscript and we can give special editorial help where an author is an authority on his subject but an inexperienced writer. We are rigorously selective in the choice of books we publish. We set the highest standards of editorial quality and accuracy. This means that a *Paperfront* is easy to understand and delightful to read. Where illustrations are necessary to convey points of detail, these are drawn up by a subject specialist artist from our panel.

HOW WE KEEP PRICES LOW

We aim for the big seller. This enables us to order enormous print runs and achieve the lowest price for you. Unfortunately, this means that you will not find in the *Paperfront* list any titles on obscure subjects of minority interest only. These could not be printed in large enough quantities to be sold for the low price at which we offer this series.

We sell almost all our *Paperfronts* at the same unit price. This saves a lot of fiddling about in our clerical departments and helps us to give you world-beating value. Under this system, the longer titles are offered at a price which we believe to be unmatched by any publisher in the world.

OUR DISTRIBUTION SYSTEM

Because or the competitive price, and the rapid turnover, *Paperfronts* are possibly the most profitable line a bookseller can handle. They are stocked by the best bookshops all over the world. It may be that your bookseller has run out of stock of a particular title. If so, he can order more from us at any time—we have a fine reputation for "same day" despatch, and we supply any order, however small (even a single copy), to any bookseller who has an account with us. We prefer you to buy from your bookseller, as this reminds him of the strong underlying public demand for *Paperfronts*. Members of the public who live in remote places, or who are housebound, or whose local bookseller is unco-operative, can order direct from us by post.

FREE

If you would like an up-to-date list of all the paperfront titles currently available, send a stamped self-addressed envelope to
ELLIOT RIGHT WAY BOOKS, BRIGHTON RD.,
LOWER KINGSWOOD, SURREY, U.K.